TILTING THE PLAYING FIELD

TILTING THE PLAYING FIELD

SCHOOLS, SPORTS, SEX AND TITLE IX

Jessica Gavora

ENCOUNTER BOOKS
SAN FRANCISCO

First edition published in 2002 by Encounter Books, an activity of Encounter for Culture and Education, Inc., a nonprofit tax exempt corporation.

Encounter Books website address: www.encounterbooks.com

Manufactured in the United States and printed on acid-free paper.

The paper used in this publication meets the minimum requirements of ANSI/NISO Z39.48-1992 (R 1997)(*Permanence of Paper*).

FIRST EDITION

Library of Congress Cataloging-in-Publication Data

Gavora, Jessica.
    Tilting the playing field : schools, sports, sex and Title IX/Jessica Gavora.—1st ed.
    p. cm.
    Includes bibliographical references (p.) and index.
    ISBN 1-893554-35-X (alk. paper)
    Sports for women—United States. 2. Sex discrimination in sports—United States. 3. Sex discrimination in education—United States. 4. Women athletes—Government Policy—United States. I Title.

    GV709.18.U6 G38 2002
    796'.082—dc21
    2001055597

10 9 8 7 6 5 4 3 2 1

To my big brother Rudy,
who taught me how to play like a boy.

CONTENTS

INTRODUCTION

THE STRONGER WOMEN GET, THE MORE THEY HATE FEMINISM

*If you grew up female in America, you heard this: Sports
are unfeminine. And this: Girls who play sports are
tomboys or lesbians. You got this message: Real women
don't spend their free time sliding feet-first into home plate
or smacking their fists into soft leather gloves.*
　　　　　　　　—Mariah Burton Nelson, *The Stronger
　　　　　　　　　Women Get, the More Men Love Football*

I N 1972, I WAS AN AWKWARD, outsized fourth-grader, pushing six feet
tall. Boys had little use for me, and I was an uninspired student.
What saved me was sports.

Basketball, to be exact. I could catch a basketball with one hand
(the ability to "palm" the ball would come a year later, in fifth grade).
Basketball was what I could do—what I thought I was *meant* to do.
My brother Rudy and I played hours of one-on-one underneath the
hoop in front of our house in Fairbanks, Alaska. Rudy was bigger and
older than I was, but I still occasionally managed to inspire a breath-
less "nice shot!" from him. And I learned a lot from the competition
he provided. So when the opportunity came along to play "organized" ball at Joy Elementary School in 1972, I grabbed it.

If you've ever seen fourth-grade girls play basketball, you know
there was actually nothing organized about our game. Turnovers
were constant, the refs couldn't keep up with the fouls and calls for
traveling, and dramatic fast breaks were often mistakenly scored at
the team's own basket. Still, my girlfriends and I took basketball seriously and spent our precious recesses practicing in the gym while the
rest of our classmates took to the swings and monkey bars outside.

We had no idea (nor, I suspect, did our teachers) that a law had
just been passed in Washington, D.C.— still a long way from Fairbanks back in 1972—guaranteeing the right of fourth-grade girls to

play basketball. Perhaps it was just something to do during those long Alaskan winters; but whatever the reason, I was blessed that year to begin an athletic career that enriched my life in ways I am only now beginning to realize.

I played basketball devotedly, fanatically, every year for the next nine years. Although my sports career never went beyond high school, it taught me invaluable lessons for successful adulthood: How to push myself hard—and go farther than I ever thought I could. How to be magnanimous in success and dignified in failure. How to work as part of a team. How to keep enjoying the benefits of physical fitness long after the effortless energy of youth is gone.

Now that I have grown up, lost my inside game and become an occasional critic of contemporary feminism, I am often approached by people (usually women) who remind me that I, like other young American women, stand on the shoulders of earlier generations of feminists. I am told that the kinds of opportunities I had at Joy Elementary School were not guaranteed but won by the sacrifices of women who went before me. And I take these admonitions seriously. In fact, I am grateful to have grown up in a country and at a time when my interests and ambitions, however much against the grain, were supported and encouraged. I would not have been happy in a world that forced me to be a dancer or a cheerleader when I really wanted to play basketball; nor would I want my own daughter to inherit such a world.

Like other women my age and younger, I grew up with an almost limitless sense of opportunity. Yet I have become aware that the women's movement we inherited, though claiming to support our liberation, fails to share our optimism and confidence. Instead of reflecting and, indeed, reveling in our expanded horizons, the feminism of the National Organization for Women and other so-called "women's groups" is oddly suspicious of our experience. It depicts women as passive victims rather than the makers of their own destinies, and overlooks our individuality in favor of a collective political identity that many of us find restrictive.

THIS IS A BOOK ABOUT THE American women's movement in the past quarter-century and about the origins and consequences of one of its most important tools: an ever-mutating federal law called Title IX. Congress did a seemingly simple and laudable thing in 1972 when it passed Title IX, saying that government could no longer discriminate between men and women in spending money on education.

But as columnist George Will has written, legislators don't pass laws, they pass sentiments; and it's up to bureaucrats and courts to say how those sentiments will be honored. This has certainly been the case with Title IX. More than any other federal law, it has been interpreted and twisted and bent outside the institutions of our electoral democracy. Congress got the ball rolling in 1972, but it was in the faculty lounges and women's conferences, in the federal bureaucracies and courtrooms of America that Title IX morphed into its present form.

The story of this law is in many ways the story of the women's movement. In 1972, American feminism was arguably reaching its apex. As Betty Friedan had urged nine years earlier in *The Feminine Mystique,* women were casting off the chains of home and husband and entering the workforce in record numbers. The notion that a higher education was "wasted" on women was rapidly becoming stigmatized, for the professional and business roles that women increasingly were expected to hold transformed a college education from a luxury to a necessity.

Congress responded by passing the Equal Rights Act and, later that same year, Title IX. The sentiment that most members of Congress sought to express in Title IX was equality under the law—nothing more and nothing less. Discrimination against women in admissions to universities and graduate schools was real in many areas and had been documented in congressional hearings. It would no longer be permitted.

Title IX, then, was the institutionalization of formal equality, but it was also the codification of feminism. American women's sense of entitlement had exploded since the 1960s, and they were demanding, and beginning to receive, the right to go to college and graduate school on the same footing as men. For politically symbolic reasons as much as anything else—a way of catching up to a movement that was already way ahead of it—Congress moved to go on record as outlawing discrimination on the basis of sex in the educational institutions and programs it funded.

For the next decade, the focus of the feminist movement was not Title IX but ratification of the Equal Rights Amendment. When the clock ran out on the ERA at midnight on June 30, 1982, feminists found themselves three states short of the thirty-eight needed to add the amendment to the Constitution; so they looked elsewhere for a vehicle to achieve their goals. "What we need to do, in the absence of a national mandate and clear policy statement, is to apply and defend the progress that has been made and to develop tools to take the profit and habit out of sexual discrimination," said Phyllis N. Segal, legal director of the National Organization for Women's Legal Defense and Education Fund, just days after the failure to ratify the ERA.[1]

And the "tool" whose scope and impact had been least explored, all agreed, was Title IX. Many of the gains that feminists had hoped to secure with the ERA, they saw, could be achieved through expansion and manipulation of the law against sex discrimination. Gender-proportional outcomes could be guaranteed, if not in employment, then in the equally critical area of education. Thus was launched a campaign to turn Title IX from an anti-discrimination statute into what the *New York Times* called a "far-reaching remedial tool" for women.[2]

THE PHRASE "UNINTENDED CONSEQUENCES" is a familiar one in the debate over the excesses of the modern bureaucratic state. Typically it is invoked to explain why a well-intended government program or policy has somehow gone terribly awry—for example, how a policy of open-ended, no-questions-asked welfare benefits encouraged illegitimacy and dependence. But perhaps nowhere in the litany of second thoughts about the nanny state are "unintended consequences" invoked more often than in reference to Title IX. To be exact, a law designed to end discrimination against women is now causing discrimination against men.

The dictates of gender politics are such that the brave public official who dares to utter a negative word about Title IX must be careful to confine his or her criticism to its "unintended consequences." These artfully worded statements often begin with sweeping tributes to the law and the progress it has ostensibly yielded for women. Only later—in suddenly small, halting voices—do the critics express qualms about the law's application. Title IX should not be implemented as a "quota law," they say. Quotas are bad, as even the most radical practitioner of identity politics acknowledges. Quotas are also the squid's ink of any discussion of race or gender, the term whose mere mention clouds the issue in such a way that the advocate of preferences gets away with his or her commitment intact. Of course we are all against quotas!

And so the preponderance of what the public hears about Title IX today focuses on the positive, the heroic, the groundbreaking. It seems that a woman cannot be successful in athletics without that success being attributed not to her talent and dedication, but to a federal law. Thus the members of the U.S. Women's World Cup soccer team, who won a stunning victory over China in 1999, are "the daughters of Title IX." Likewise, Sheryl Swoopes, Kym Hampton, Rebecca Lobo and the other stars of the Women's National Basketball Association are not merely great athletes and fierce competitors, but also the embodiment of the beneficiaries of a federal law. The fact that portraying these remarkable athletes as creatures of entitlement—the welfare queens of the sports world—diminishes their achievement never seems to occur to those feminists who use them for a political agenda.

Still, these efforts to tie all women's athletic achievement to Title IX find a receptive audience in the proud moms and dads of multiplying hordes of pigtailed soccer players today—especially the dads, who are now just as able to live vicariously through their daughters' athletic exploits as those of their sons. To them, giving these energetic, bright-eyed little competitors an equal chance to kick a ball or swing a bat is an unassailable good, one that is beyond question in polite society.

Title IX has acquired sweeping jurisdiction over all aspects of education, from kindergarten to graduate school, including test scoring, housing facilities, sexual harassment and teenage pregnancy. When the law was passed, few people—least of all the original congressional sponsors—were concerned about increasing opportunities for women to row crew and play basketball. They had in mind more prosaic educational benefits like admission to schools and programs, access to financial aid and career opportunities.

Nonetheless, it has been in sports—intercollegiate sports in particular—that Title IX has won its greatest notoriety. Here too is where the law has been molded into something quite different from what its congressional sponsors intended.

Sports, of course, are unique in the American educational experience: while coeducation has become the norm in the classroom, sexual segregation still reigns on the playing field. Educational institutions routinely and without controversy set up separate programs, provide separate facilities and in some cases hire separate administrative staff for girls and boys and men and women in athletics. Doing the same thing for, say, an English department or a drama or dance program would be unthinkable. In fact, it would be illegal.

It could be argued that Congress contradicted the very principle of nondiscrimination it was trying to promote when it allowed for separate athletic teams for men and women under Title IX. Moreover, applying a law that outlaws discrimination on the basis of sex to an activity that accepts discrimination on the basis of sex has cast the most difficult issues of "gender equity" in stark relief. How can the law guarantee that men and women receive the "same opportunity" when they compete on different teams and even in different sports? How can fairness be measured? Are men and women different when it comes to sports? Do they have different levels of interest? Of ability? Do they share the same zeal for competition? The same need for hierarchy and organized, team activity?

Feminist supporters of Title IX have answered these difficult questions by trying to have it both ways: separate and equal—or, as I will argue, more than equal. In this respect, they have committed themselves to a great compromise of their own. Whereas in every other area of life, from the military to the boardroom to the bedroom, women's rights activists have insisted that women be allowed to compete in the same arena with men, Title IX activists have worked in athletics to protect women's special status. They implicitly acknowledge that if women were forced to compete with men for positions on the playing field, very few would make the cut. On this narrow score, difference is accepted. But on every other count, sameness is insisted upon, and it is from this dubious premise that Title IX has come to have such an unsettling impact on athletics.

The gender-quota logic of Title IX is inexorable. It begins with the presumption that men and women, boys and girls are identical in their athletic interests, equally eager to kick a soccer ball or wield an oar. And if interests are equal, then "equity" between men and women dictates that actual participation must also be equal. There must be just as many girl athletes per capita at any given school as there are boy athletes. Anything less is prima facie proof that someone is being discriminated against.

But once accepted, why must this logic end at the playing field's edge? Should our law then mandate that men and women attend medical school in equal numbers? Earn degrees in math and physics? What about teaching? Must we limit the number of women who can enter the education field in the interests of "gender equity"? And what of engineering? Should we use the full weight and authority of the federal government to ensure that women get a break in qualifying to be the bridge builders and software designers of tomorrow?

IT IS PART OF THE WEIRD IRONY of the identity politics currently pervading our public life that preferences for girls and women are being expanded in education at the same time that females are succeeding in American schools as never before. Far from being held back by vestigial discrimination in academia, girls and women from kindergarten to graduate school are thriving. They increasingly dominate in universities and graduate schools. And on virtually every indicia of academic achievement, they outshine boys and men. With few exceptions, they outperform, outscore and out-graduate their male counterparts in the nation's education system.

But feminists have seized on the few areas in which males have an edge over females—such as standardized test scores and participation in high-level math and science courses—to justify expanded Title IX quotas in education. As might be expected, Title IX activists have taken the presumption of sameness that holds for sports and applied it to math and science and other traditionally male-dominated fields. Here, as in sports, the definition of "equity" promoted under Title IX is not equal opportunity but equal outcomes. And here, as in sports, what feminists seek is not expanded opportunities for females to prove their mettle vis-à-vis males, but preferences for girls and women in an educational system they continue to view as dominated by "patriarchal oppression."

The National Women's Law Center (NWLC), for example, filed a complaint against the New York City school system in 2001 charging that it violated Title IX because the city's vocational high schools were segregated by sex. Nine of the city's eighteen vocational high schools, the NWLC pointed out, were over 70 percent male and four were over 70 percent female. The majority-male schools offered "many high-tech programs that lead to high-wage work" like computer repair and mechanical engineering, while the majority-female schools focused on programs leading to jobs like cosmetology, nursing assistance and clerical support. To correct the "inequities" and comply with the law, the NWLC demanded, majority-female schools like the Fashion Industries High School in Manhattan must offer more courses geared toward high-tech careers. Majority-male schools like the Aviation High School in Queens and Transit Tech High School in Brooklyn, meanwhile, must increase female enrollment and do more to make girls feel "welcome."[3]

In such fashion the twin fallacies that underlie quotas in athletics are gradually creeping into the academy: first, that disproportionate participation means something is "wrong"; and second, that the presence of correct numbers means everything is "right." Moreover, as the old-fashioned, more blatant forms of sex discrimination have disappeared from the scene, women's groups have invented new ones against which to bring the power of Title IX. Chief among these today is sexual harassment, the area of greatest expansion of the law in schools.

It used to be that women complained about what's known as "quid pro quo" harassment in the workplace and, occasionally, at school. This was easy to identify because typically it involved a male in a position of power demanding that a (usually female) subordinate submit sexually or suffer the consequences. Quid pro quo sexual harassment isn't gone, of course, but its seriousness has been undermined by a postmodern definition of sexual harassment that is less quantifiable and less easily identifiable. In the workplace, the feminist term of art for it is "hostile work environment." This can result from speech, pictures, memos, looks—just about anything that might be deemed offensive by the female "victim," even if no objective consequences of such victimization can be defined. Academia has a similar construct, often dubbed the "chilly classroom climate," generated by anything from a majority of men in a classroom or a program to the unconscious propensity of teachers to call on noisy boys more often than on reticent girls. These "microinequities" are now a major focus of women's groups seeking to expand Title IX into academia.

BUT WHY, IT MIGHT BE ASKED, should any of this Title IX business worry us at all? Girls and women suffered centuries of discrimination and lack of opportunity, so isn't it a good thing that they now have a leg up in our schools and universities? And don't we have an obligation to protect our gains, to guard against backsliding, and to ferret out discrimination and restrictions on opportunity where they remain?

As Christina Hoff Sommers noted in the opening pages of her seminal book *Who Stole Feminism?* American women do indeed owe a great debt to those leaders of the women's movement who fought to break down barriers to the full and equal participation of women in American life. That we have not only won these opportunities but also taken full advantage of them to realize our potential as women has been good—not just for individual women but for workplaces, communities and families.

That being said, it must also be remembered that the contemporary women's movement is now entering its fifth decade. A baby girl born the year Title IX was passed will be thirty this year. She grew up in a country where her rights were protected and, more importantly, she came of age in a society where her equality was overwhelmingly accepted and respected. She and the other women born in 1972 are now the parents, teachers, coaches, professors and administrators who control our educational institutions. In short, they are full participants in the "system" that Title IX feminists still assert is routinely and systematically victimizing them.

The current interpretation of Title IX, I will argue, is at odds with the experience of the women who have grown up since the law was passed. Questioning its wisdom is of a piece with questions raised in the last decade by Sommers and others about the relevance of the modern feminist movement to the vast majority of American women. Do the activists who are leading the fight for Title IX quotas really represent the grievances, wishes and aspirations of the majority of American women? Are girls and women really, as the law has been twisted to assume, identical in their interests and abilities to boys and men? Are we as likely to want to kick a ball or take a physics class? Should the law penalize men if we are not?

Questioning what has come to be known as the struggle for "gender equity" is considered sex treason by the hardcore feminists who dominate the women's movement. But I believe that women should welcome a close scrutiny of this gender obsession and what it is bringing to sports and education. And not just because boys and men—our sons and husbands and brothers—are finding themselves on the losing end of a federal regulatory regime that now officially prefers women, although that occurs with depressing regularity. What should be of greater concern to those who care about equal opportunity for girls and women is the implicit message of Title IX today: that young girls aren't worthy of respect and admiration unless and until they act like young boys. Playing sports and studying the hard sciences, those who enforce the law tell us, are worthier than the interests women have traditionally pursued. And to make sure no one misses the point, this message is backed up by real advantages in funding and resource allocation for girls and women who act accordingly—and by just as real penalties for boys and men. The losers aren't just males but also the millions of females whose talents and interests lie outside those dictated by the affirmative androgyny of the law.

ONE SPRING DAY IN WASHINGTON a couple of years ago I taped a television show on U.S. women's soccer and Title IX with a leader of the pro-quota women's movement. The show was no more contentious than others I had done on the topic. My fellow panelist and I disagreed diametrically on the impact that Title IX is having not just on sports, but on other areas of education as well. Our conversation was combative, but civil. She made her points and I made mine.

After the taping I walked out of the studio in silence with the older woman, a veteran of years of fighting for the feminist cause. As we got to our cars she suddenly stopped and turned to me. "Jessica, I'm going to say something to you that someone should have said a long time ago." She took on a stern, matronly tone and said, "You don't have any idea of the damage you're doing to women. Someday I hope you'll understand the irresponsibility of the things you are saying."

"If you have a quarrel with the points I made and the facts I presented, why didn't you make it when the cameras were rolling, instead of trying to intimidate me in the parking lot?" I said. And I got into my car.

I drove away feeling good, both about the argument I had made and about the fact that I had stood up to a more seasoned competitor. The lessons I learned from being an athlete—how to be confident and independent, to trust my abilities and strive for excellence—had stood me in good stead. I was my own woman.

ONE

THE NUMBERS GAME

Intent, as history shows, is a poor bulwark against despotism.
                            —Mark Helprin

W HEN THE U.S. TEAM kicked its way to a spectacular victory over China in the Women's World Cup soccer final in the summer of 1999, the win was hailed as not just a triumph for women's soccer, but a triumph for women. Cynthia McFadden of ABC News proclaimed Mia Hamm, Brandi Chastain and the other members of the U.S. team "the heiresses of the women's movement." *Newsweek*'s Jonathan Alter announced a new era for women. In the women's soccer team, he gushed, feminism had "a new comfortable place" to reside. *USA Today* looked forward hopefully to the election of "President Chastain" in 2016, and then to 2055 as "the year college football was eliminated due to lack of interest."

The U.S. women's soccer team was indeed a sensation in the summer of 1999, drawing the kind of audiences and endorsement deals normally reserved for men's professional sports figures. It didn't hurt that they were winning, of course. Nor did it hurt that they were all attractive young women, an image cultivated by Chastain posing semi-nude in the pages of the men's magazine *Gear*.

But it was, from the beginning, more than a sports story. Politicians and media commentators couldn't talk about the women's soccer team that summer without also talking about politics. The *Denver Post* dubbed the U.S. women's success "the revenge of the soccer moms." Former Colorado congresswoman Pat Schroeder said the American lady booters had "provided little girls with a picture of the millennium woman—a woman who is self-confident and capable of excelling in anything she chooses to do." The connection between women's soccer and women's rights became so fixed in the media that a year later the *Washington Post* sought to gauge the status of women in Brazil by the popularity—or lack thereof—of the Brazilian women's soccer team. "The attitude here toward women's soccer may concern only a game, but it is emblematic of a broader problem for Brazil, and for many other countries emerging from poverty," the *Post* reported. "What Brazil and many other developing countries are finding is that laws, progressive policies...have failed to uproot the enduring traditions that constitute the biggest obstacle to women's economic progress."[1]

Back in the USA, in contrast, the quickly congealing conventional wisdom was that a "progressive public policy" had not only made life better for women but also made women better at sports. The new stage in the women's movement symbolized by the U.S. women's soccer team, Americans were told, was brought about by a law: Title IX of the Education Amendments of 1972.

Sensing a photo opportunity, politicians of all kinds moved quickly to associate themselves with the act of legislation that brought us the camera-ready "girls of summer." President Bill Clinton hosted the U.S. women's soccer team at the White House and thanked Title IX for giving "millions and millions and millions of girls" the message "that they can follow their dreams." Jesse Jackson affirmed the connection between gender and race and legislatively mandated opportunity: "Without Title IX and without affirmative action, those women would not have been on the field," he declared. And when Republicans in the U.S. House of Representatives tried to push through a resolution congratulating the women's soccer team without including the obligatory obeisance to Title IX, Democrats cried foul. "They are simply in a state of denial with regards to the national government's role," said Representative Bruce Vento, a Minnesota Democrat. "They can deny that Title IX didn't play a role [*sic*], but the fact is that it did. Only Republicans could screw up an international championship."

The World Cup couldn't have come at a better time. In the summer of 1999, the American women's movement was desperate for some good news. Membership in women's groups like the National Organization for Women was dwindling, while both men and women (to NOW's shock and horror) were flocking to the Promise Keepers, a male-centered movement that advocated a return to traditional roles for husband and wife. Even worse, feminists had just endured a thirteen-month impeachment ordeal in which they stood largely silent as a president they supported stood accused of sexual harassment and rape.[2]

The American women's big win over the Chinese team in the summer of 1999 was a chance to reverse the dismal decline of feminism. Women's groups began a media campaign to graft the success of women's soccer onto their political agenda, and journalists and commentators unquestioningly repeated their mantra: The "girls of summer" were actually the "daughters of Title IX," as *Time* called them. So complete was the identification between the team and the law, *USA Today* concluded, that Title IX was now "one of the most untouchable laws in the land."[3] The *Washington Post's* Ann Gerhart even called Brandi Chastain's black sports bra—unveiled in a dramatic act of product placement in the seconds following the World Cup victory—"the cloth symbol of Title IX's success."[4] Hamm, Chastain et al. appeared simultaneously on the covers of *Time, Newsweek, People* and *Sports Illustrated*—the new faces of confident, successful American women and the new symbols of the triumph of Title IX.

But Title IX had other faces as well, also on display in the summer of 1999, although not on the nation's front pages:

Boston, Massachusetts: As she had done to all male students for twenty-five years, self-proclaimed "radical feminist" philosophy professor Mary Daly denied sophomore Duane Naquin admission to her feminist ethics course at Boston College in the fall of 1999 on the grounds that he was a threat to the "safe, nurturing educational space" for women that her sex-segregated classroom provided. Naquin threatened to sue Boston College for discriminating against him on the basis of his sex. Barring him from Daly's class, he and his attorneys charged, was forbidden under Title IX.

But now Daly was suing back. Ironically, the basis of her complaint, too, was Title IX. And not just Title IX, according to her attorney, Gretchen Van Ness, but "the cutting edge of Title IX." Said Van Ness, "There's nothing that says what she's been doing is per se against the law. In fact, Title IX has said that when you are making up for past discrimination and have a pedagogical reason for what you're doing, it might be permissible."[5]

Dayton, Ohio: Nate Studney was a junior on the wrestling team at Miami University of Ohio when news came that the 1998 season would be the team's last. Citing a budget deficit and pressure under Title IX to achieve "gender equity" in its sports program, the university announced that it was killing men's soccer, tennis and wrestling, effective June 1. No woman at Miami had claimed she was discriminated against. No women's team had charged unequal treatment. It was simply a question of numbers. Because females comprised over 50 percent of Miami's undergraduates but only 42 percent of its athletes, the school was in danger of having "too few" women athletes—and, conversely, "too many" men—under the current interpretation of Title IX known as the "proportionality test." Something had to give. The three men's teams in question ate up just 4.7 percent of Miami's $10.5 million athletic budget, but they involved seventy athletes. Removing them would balance the numbers and create the illusion of "gender equity" at Miami—without adding a single female athlete.

"I felt discriminated against because I am a man but at the same time no women were being helped," said Studney. "It wouldn't have mattered to me if women had got more opportunities."

Providence, Rhode Island: Charlie Hickey had coached the winningest season in Providence College baseball history when his program was dropped in the spring of 1998. Panicked Providence administrators had consulted university attorneys and were advised to eliminate the 11-point gap between the percentages of female students and female athletes, and achieve "proportionality" or face a lawsuit and/or a federal investigation.

At Providence, as at Miami, fifty-seven male athletes lost their opportunity to compete and no new women's teams were added. "How crazy is it that, in order to create athletic opportunities for women, Providence College has had to take athletic opportunities away from men?" commented one local sports columnist.[6]

Lexington, North Carolina: Six-year-old Jonathan Prevette became a poster child for the excesses of political correctness when he was suspended from his elementary school for kissing a classmate on the cheek. Jonathan said the girl asked for the kiss, and she never complained to teachers. Nonetheless, school officials sprang into action. "A six-year-old kissing another six-year-old is inappropriate behavior," said a district spokeswoman. "Unwelcome is unwelcome at any age."

Politicians and commentators nationwide decried the overreaction of officials at Prevette's school, but few stopped to consider the motivation for their response: Title IX. Meeting with Prevette's parents, the principal of his school said that Jonathan's action "had the potential of becoming a problem under the district's sexual harassment policy"—a policy that Title IX requires every school to have, including elementary schools. At young Jonathan's school, as in most schools, just what constituted sexual harassment was vague. Words, gestures, pictures, even looks could form the basis for a violation of the law. And as federal officials began to insist that Title IX sexual harassment prohibitions applied not just to predatory teachers and administrators but to fellow students as well, little boys across the country joined Prevette in being labeled potential harassers.

WHAT IS TITLE IX? And how has it come to have such a broad impact on both women and men, both boys and girls in America?

For most Americans, Title IX is synonymous with women and sports. If they've heard of the law at all, it is probably from glowing press coverage: heroic tales of gutsy women taking on the male-dominated sports world and winning—stories that invariably trace the existence of successful female athletes, like those on the U.S. Women's World Cup soccer team, to Title IX. While men's success on the playing field is invariably attributed to hard work and a fierce competitive spirit, it is unusual to read a story about a successful female athlete without also reading that her success owes to Title IX.

In fact, however, the law that is credited for breaking down the barriers of entry for thousands of girls and women to the testosterone-saturated world of athletics never mentions sports at all. The crucial language of Title IX is deceptively simple and to the point:

> No person in the United States shall, on the basis of sex, be excluded from participation in, be denied the benefits of, or be subjected to discrimination under any education program or activity receiving Federal financial assistance.

Language this broad can cover a lot of ground, and Title IX does. In addition to sports, it covers admissions, student recruitment, course offerings, counseling, financial aid, housing, employment, scholarships, testing, health, pregnancy—anything and everything done by an educational institution that receives federal money in any form. It applies to public as well as private schools, and to kindergarten through graduate school. Title IX even covers government training programs, museums and private companies that receive federal education funds. In short, if it is touched by federal money and has an "educational" purpose, it falls under the jurisdiction of Title IX.

But it is sports—particularly college sports—that have made Title IX a household term.

When Heather Sue Mercer successfully sued Duke University to protest being cut from the football team, for instance, the law she used was Title IX. Coach Fred Goldsmith, Mercer charged, had discriminated against her, the only woman on the hundred-plus-man Duke squad, not because she was a lousy place kicker but because she was a woman. In fact, as Duke president Nannerl O. Keohane testified at trial, Mercer was given extra chances to make the team. Coach Goldsmith said he admired her spunk, but he and several former coaches and kickers testified that she didn't have the strength to boot long field goals against major college competition. Duke denied any bias, but the jury sided with the lady placekicker and awarded Mercer $2 million for her trouble.

In another case, when two soccer moms from California's Napa Valley were upset that their daughters were forced to play soccer in the winter while the boys' teams used the fields in the fall, they filed a complaint under Title IX. Girls, they maintained, were being treated unequally by having to play in the rain and mud after the boys had enjoyed the milder fall conditions. The federal government sent in a team of investigators and agreed, ordering school districts across a wide swath of northern California to move the girls' soccer season from winter to spring—or make the boys share equally in the chilly conditions of winter. As a result, soccer-playing girls are now complaining that they have to choose between soccer and other sports whose seasons suddenly overlap it, like softball, track and swimming. Lots of kids are upset, but the soccer moms are satisfied that they struck a blow for women's rights. "It's not a sports issue, it's a civil rights issue," one of them told the *Los Angeles Times*. "And you don't violate the law just because some kids have to make a choice."[7]

The most familiar Title IX sports scenario today, however, involves neither girls on football teams nor disgruntled soccer moms. In the fall of 2000, when the federal government ordered the University of Wisconsin at Madison to create a new women's sport—even though no women on campus were clamoring for a new sport—the authority cited was Title IX. UWM had worked hard for over a decade to comply with education bureaucrats' notion of "equity" under the law, which is defined as proportionately equal participation by men and women, regardless of interest. Women's crew and ice hockey teams were added. The men's baseball team was eliminated. In 1999 UWM officials cut the number of nonscholarship players who could "walk on" the men's teams, including the Badger football team. They instituted floors below which participation on women's teams was not allowed to drop. By the autumn of 2000, they thought they had hit the mark: an equal number of men and women played varsity sports on the Madison campus. But not so fast. Because the student body was 53 percent female and 47 percent male, the federal government decreed that the university was still twenty-five female athletes short. To comply with the law and save its federal funding, its sports program had to mirror its student body perfectly. Wisconsin had to either add a women's team or kill a men's team to make the numbers right. University officials angrily appealed the ruling. At the time of this writing, officials at the Office for Civil Rights had yet to retract their assertion that Wisconsin was guilty of discrimination against women under federal law.

Stories like this are distressingly common in intercollegiate sports today, where the proportionality test has been the reigning standard of Title IX compliance for the better part of a decade. But now a new crop of Title IX horror stories is beginning to surface outside the world of sports. Having spent a turbulent adolescence in athletics, Title IX is coming into adulthood as a law that grants women protected status in a vast and expanding universe of federally funded education.

- FairTest, an advocacy group opposed to standardized testing, enlisted the government's help under Title IX to force changes in the Preliminary Scholastic Assessment Test (PSAT) because too few National Merit Scholarship finalists (as determined by their PSAT scores) were women.
- Four Texas cheerleaders successfully used Title IX to sue their school district for being kicked off the squad because they were pregnant.
- When parents of softball players at Merritt Island High School in Florida noticed that the boys' baseball field was nicer than the girls' softball field, they sued the school district under Title IX. The boys, it was true, had better grass, big bleachers, a concession stand and scoreboards. But the reason was not because the school district had paid for them, but because baseball parents and supporters volunteered their time and money. Still, the court ordered that wherever the resources came from, the facilities had to be equal for girls and boys. That meant the boys' baseball "Home of the Mustangs" sign had to be painted over because the girls didn't have one.

In its three decades of existence, Title IX has had a profound—and for increasing numbers of observers a profoundly disturbing—impact on American life. Yet for its supporters, the problem is not too much but too little Title IX. Surveying the landscape in 2000, the American Association of University Women, one of the most zealous advocacy groups for the law, lamented that Title IX has yet to reach its full potential as a tool to transform American education. Triumphs on the playing field, said the AAUW, "overshadow Title IX's much broader mandate to eliminate sex discrimination in all areas of publicly funded education. Title IX is the shoehorn meant to guarantee girls and women access to higher education and career education, better employment opportunities, increased opportunities in mathematics and science, protection against sexual harassment, standardized testing that is free of gender bias, and fair treatment of pregnant and parenting students."[8]

LIKE THE LAWS TO PROTECT the civil rights of blacks passed years before it, Title IX began as a simple anti-discrimination statute that had a powerful and necessary, if sometimes symbolic, effect on American education. As a matter of fact, Title IX was patterned after Title VI of the Civil Rights Act of 1964, which outlawed discrimination on the basis of race, color or national origin in government-funded programs. Except for the substitution of the word "sex" in Title IX for "race, color or national origin" in Title VI, the two statutes use identical language to describe the benefited class. Both laws also provide the same administrative mechanism for terminating federal financial support to institutions engaged in prohibited discrimination.

In the 1960s and 1970s millions of women moved into the workforce, and simultaneously entered higher education in greater numbers. This trend, it is important to note at the outset, began well before the passage of Title IX. Women increased from 25 percent of undergraduates in 1950 to 43 percent in 1971, the year before the law was passed.[9] Still, barriers remained. Some colleges and universities had dual-track admissions policies that openly required higher academic qualifications for women than for men. Congress heard testimony from women's groups that quotas limiting the admission of women were common. Women shared anecdotes about losing financial aid when they got married, or being accused of merely "marking time" in universities and graduate schools until they inevitably had children and abandoned any pretence of life outside the family.

As the women's movement grew in force and sophistication—a

growth fueled, ironically, by the increased female presence in higher education that preceded Title IX—the pressure on Congress to fully open the doors of America's schools to girls and women increased. Senator Birch Bayh, the Senate sponsor of Title IX, insisted that legislation was needed "to provide women with solid legal protection from the persistent, pernicious discrimination which is serving to perpetuate second-class citizenship for American women." Yet when Congress began to debate legislation outlawing discrimination on the basis of sex in federally funded educational institutions, much of the debate centered on members' fears of the institutionalization of sex quotas under the law. Professor Julian H. Levi of the University of Chicago, in a letter to the Senate Judiciary Committee, pointed to "the temptation in these matters for the examining agents to turn to a statistical report and then, purely on the basis of percentages, to thrust the burden upon the institution. This has resulted in some places responding somewhat akin to the reasoning in the busing cases, that past discrepancies now justify reverse discrimination." Even the *New York Times* weighed in against the bill, ironically evoking a now lost notion of educational "diversity": "[The bill] tells the colleges that if they admit any substantial number of the other sex, they have lost control of their admission policy," editorialized the *Times*. "Henceforth, to receive any federal aid, they have to admit students of both sexes on an equal basis.... A truly humane politics, call it liberalism or conservatism, would help a society protect diversity. But here the power of the law is again used to make life less diverse."

Bayh and other supporters of Title IX, like the congressional sponsors of the Civil Rights Act eight years earlier, promised that nothing in the law would lead to sex quotas in schools. But skittish congressmen, remembering when Senator Hubert Humphrey promised to eat the pages of the 1964 Civil Rights Act if it turned out to allow "preferential treatment for any group," demanded the same protection in Title IX that Humphrey had included in the Civil Rights Act. So Representative Albert Quie, a Minnesota Republican, added a clause to the bill taken almost word for word from the Civil Rights Act, a provision designed to ensure that "no college will be required to give preferential treatment to any person solely on the basis of sex so as to balance an existing imbalance within the composition of the student body." In June 1972, Congress passed Title IX, complete with this caveat:

Nothing [in the law] shall be interpreted to require any educational institution to grant preferential or disparate treatment to the members of one sex on account of an imbalance which may exist with respect to the total number or percentage of persons of that sex participating in or receiving the benefits of any federally supported program or activity, in comparison with the total number or percentage of persons of that sex in any community, State, section, or other area.

In other words, what later happened to the Providence College baseball team and the Miami University of Ohio wrestling team in 1998 under Title IX was not intended to happen. Athletic directors and university administrators were not supposed to be forced to grant preferences to women or discriminate against men in order to correct a gender "imbalance" in their programs. If their athletic squads failed to mirror the male-female proportions of their student bodies, so be it. A Title IX gap, Congress said in 1972, is okay as long as it isn't produced by discrimination on the basis of sex.

And if Congress never intended to force schools to eliminate male athletes in the name of creating opportunity for female athletes, it surely never intended to allow Mary Daly to close the doors of her classroom to men in order to compensate, as she claimed, for previous discrimination against women. The words of the statute outlawing discrimination "on the basis of sex" don't specify *which* sex; they apply equally to men and women. And yet under the spreading umbrella of Title IX, Daly and other pro-preference feminists routinely seek to justify discrimination on the basis of sex—against men. Such discrimination is not only justified, they contend, it's *required* to compensate women for the wrongs they have suffered in the past.

FEMINISTS HAVE NOT BEEN SHY about pushing for preferences for women under Title IX because the law's interpretation has been shaped by the movement for affirmative action—despite the changes Congress included to prohibit quotas. By the late Sixties, feminists had begun to be inspired by African-Americans who increasingly called for affirmative efforts by government to equalize employment and educational achievement when the end of legal discrimination in the mid-Sixties failed to bring about the swift advances its advocates had predicted. They were demanding (to paraphrase Lyndon Johnson, their advocate in this regard) some extra help not only in starting, but also in finishing and winning the race for the American Dream, some "affirmative action" on the part of government to remedy the wounds of history. Women, too, had been hobbled by a history of discrimination and oppression, the early supporters of Title IX believed. How could they now be expected to compete equally with the men who had oppressed them and gained such a head start? For these early gender feminists, freedom was not enough. Justice for women required that government act affirmatively to give them a preference in education. The social forces arrayed against women were too strong and too well entrenched to simply level the playing field and expect women to compete with men.

The government-granted preference that inspired women's activists to push for affirmative action in Title IX was an executive order issued by President Lyndon Johnson in 1965. Recognized as the dawning of the era of affirmative action, Executive Order 11246 obligated federal contractors to devise preference plans that had "the result of assuring that there was minority group representation in all trades on the job in all phases of the work."[10] In 1968, Johnson amended Executive Order 11246 to include sex as a criterion for "minority group."

Bernice Sandler was the first person to realize that Executive Order 11246 could be used to help open the doors of colleges and universities to women. A part-time lecturer at the University of Maryland, Sandler applied in 1969 for a full-time faculty position at the university and was rejected. A friend on the faculty told her that although her qualifications were excellent, she "came on too strong for a woman." Stung, Sandler set about getting even.

Inspired by the developing system of race-based affirmative action that was growing up around Executive Order 11246, Sandler went to work with a group called the Women's Equity Action League (WEAL) and a friendly Department of Labor official to win similar preferences for women. They managed to file federal complaints against more than 250 colleges and universities—including every medical school in the country—complaining that they had too few women on their faculties. They generated letter campaigns to the Department of Labor and to members of Congress, and made sure the press knew what they were up to. Eventually, Sandler and WEAL attracted an ally on the Hill. In the early summer of 1970, Congresswoman Edith Green of Oregon, a member of WEAL's advisory board, held the first hearings on what would eventually become Title IX.

"Edith Green was smart," says Sandler. "She didn't let us lobby for this bill. We came to her and said, 'What can we do?' And she said, 'Nothing. Nobody knows what's in this bill. And if you start making noise about it, they'll ask.'"

So they didn't make any noise about it, and very few people asked. Testifying at the Green hearings were Sandler, other WEAL members, representatives of the National Organization for Women and members of the Nixon administration. As the main witness, Sandler argued that women, like blacks, needed "a compensatory kind of push" to recover from past discrimination. "It is completely inconsistent to say that a particular minority ought to get...help in getting into college, when it turns out quite often that the members of that particular minority, be it black, Mexican American or whatever, more often than not tend to be practically all males," she testified. The NOW representative called for the implementation of the "first and only living Affirmative Action Program" for women in colleges and universities. Subcommittee chairwoman Green herself argued that statistics alone provided proof of discrimination: "The Federal Government has shown the absence of Negroes in a classroom to be in and of itself proof of discrimination," she told the hearing. "It seems to me the same criteria should be used insofar as women are concerned."

No representative of higher education testified at the Green hearings. "They were asked," says Sandler. "The Green committee called the American Council on Education—the lobbying arm of higher ed—and they said, 'Oh there's no sex discrimination in higher education, and besides, it's not a problem.' That's a quote."

Shelley Steinbach, who monitored federal developments for the American Council on Education in the 1970s, acknowledges that higher education "did not engage in extensively vigilant observation of what was going on" as Title IX was being passed by Congress. Preoccupied with what they considered more pressing issues, and satisfied that the protections against quotas built into the bill would work, representatives of the nation's colleges and universities remained on the sidelines in 1972.

BY JULY 1972 WOMEN'S GROUPS had their law, but it was far from the pro-preference mandate they had hoped it would be. Sandler and other women's activists, however, were in it for the long haul. They understood that many opportunities to shape Title IX were yet to come.

"You start with a law," says Sandler. "But then you have to see that the law gets interpreted through the regulations and through the courts correctly—or the way you would like it. And then it's seeing that the regulation and the law get enforced by the courts and the Department of Education. It's seeing that people know about it so they know their rights. And it's seeing if there are new areas that we need to look at for enforcement under the law."

Although the Ford administration Department of Health, Education and Welfare (HEW) published implementing regulations for Title IX in 1975, the regulations were vague and provided no guidance to schools on how to enforce the law against sex discrimination in athletics. The result was that HEW was flooded with complaints from confused colleges and universities struggling to comply with Title IX in their sports programs. So officials went back to the drawing board. Women's groups were invited to collaborate with what were now Carter administration HEW bureaucrats in writing new regulations to "clarify" how Title IX should be applied to athletic programs. Sandler and other women's activists formed an informal working group that worked closely first with Ford administration and later with Carter administration Department of Education officials. They also created the National Coalition for Women and Girls in Education (NCWGE) to lobby for the regulations before Congress.

"A good analogy to use is the 'hide the ball' technique," says Steinbach of the collaboration between sympathetic Carter administration officials and women's groups as the Title IX athletics regulations were being drafted. "This was the number one issue on their agenda. They cared. They had people inside the administration who cared, fellow traveler types. And they were kept abreast of what was going on. Nobody ever called me and said, 'Shelley, you know your schools are about to get screwed? Get in here and do something.' No phone call like that ever occurred. Phone calls of the other kind always occurred."

This collaboration between women's groups and Education Department officials eventually produced what is known as the 1979 Title IX Athletics Policy Interpretation. Although the Policy Interpretation lacks the legal status of an official government regulation, it nonetheless has been treated by succeeding administrations and by the courts as the government's final word on implementing Title IX in athletics. For preference advocates like Sandler, the document represented a great leap toward the version of Title IX that they had always advocated. For it was here—in an interpretation written pursuant to the 1975 regulation that was itself written pursuant to the actual 1972 law—that the requirement that males and females participate in sports at equal rates was first articulated.

The 1979 document sets out a three-part test to measure a school's compliance with Title IX. The first and most important of these tests (as I'll later explore in detail) is whether the gender balance of a school's athletic program mirrors that of the student body. Sandler and the other women who worked with Department of Education officials in writing the Policy Interpretation would have preferred that it go further and directly mandate a 50/50 gender ratio of participation in sports. Still, by focusing on the proportions of the student body, not any presumed discrimination, they had succeeded in fundamentally changing how the federal government would enforce the law.

Congress has never amended Title IX in the years since 1972, but clearly, thanks to the 1979 Policy Interpretation and the hard work of groups like the Women's Equity Action League, the law has been changed to more resemble the keen-edged tool that Bernice Sandler and others envisioned in 1969. The discrimination that was once explicitly prohibited by Congress is now, paradoxically, widely accepted to be the measure of nondiscrimination against women in intercollegiate sports. A law that was once meant to guarantee equal opportunity is now construed to guarantee equal outcomes. And the guarantee of equal outcomes that has taken root in athletics under Title IX is now spreading to other areas of education.

LEO KOCHER, ASSOCIATE PROFESSOR and head wrestling coach at the University of Chicago, suspected something was very wrong in intercollegiate sports when Drake University suddenly decided to drop its wrestling program in 1993. The Drake program was the 110th wrestling team to be cut by a college or university in a decade. If the trend continued, Kocher concluded, wrestling would disappear from intercollegiate athletics in a matter of years.

"I already knew that wrestling in college had proportionately fewer programs compared to the number of high school programs," says Kocher, a longtime follower of Title IX. "I looked at the numbers and found that for every NCAA college wrestling program there were about thirty-two high schools that wrestled. Then I compared it to a sport like soccer in which for every NCAA program there were about ten high school programs. It struck me as strange that you would have all this demand at the high school level and colleges weren't meeting that demand. It made me wonder why."

The answer was Title IX. For advocates of gender quotas, 1993 was the beginning of a period of stepped-up enforcement of the law based on the 1979 "proportionality test"—a period of enforcement that would complete Title IX's transformation from the equal opportunity statute passed in 1972.

The most visible sign of the new era was in the federal bureaucracy. Newly elected President Bill Clinton had appointed as his chief Title IX enforcer Norma Cantu, a fourteen-year veteran of the Mexican-American Legal Defense and Education Fund (MALDEF). Cantu's penchant for using the courts to extract preferences for her clients led civil rights attorney Clint Bolick to dub her, along with Clinton Justice Department civil rights nominee Lani Guinier, "Clinton's Quota Queens." But while the title stuck to Guinier and contributed to the withdrawal of her nomination, Cantu sailed through Senate confirmation without a single dissenting vote.

Safely ensconced atop a seven-hundred-member staff and a $60 million budget, Cantu quickly moved to mold the Education Department's Office for Civil Rights (OCR) in her own image. Under Cantu, the office promised to end the "reactive approach to civil rights enforcement" of the Reagan and Bush administrations and put in place a "proactive" enforcement regime. While Republican administrations had contented themselves with investigating civil rights complaints as they came into the office from schools and universities, Cantu's crew would emphasize "agency-initiated investigations." That is, instead of waiting for trouble to come to them, they would go out and look for it. In the first nineteen months of Cantu's tenure, OCR began 240 reviews of schools from which no civil rights complaints had been filed. In addition, she instructed her ten regional offices to double the number of complaints they investigated—in effect setting a goal for Title IX actions.

AT THE SAME TIME THAT Cantu and her coterie of activist federal enforcers were arriving in Washington, the federal courts were taking the first steps toward mandating gender quotas in athletics. The major motivating force was a landmark Supreme Court ruling in 1992, *Franklin v. Gwinnett County Public Schools,* which for the first time made monetary damages available to Title IX plaintiffs. Lawsuits alleging discrimination on the basis of sex exploded in colleges and universities. Eager trial lawyers and women's groups scoured the country for aggrieved female athletes, and found them—or manufactured them.

In the months following *Franklin,* female soccer players at Auburn University filed a class action lawsuit charging they were being discriminated against because the university would not elevate their team to fully funded varsity status. At Colgate University, Jennifer Cook and four of her teammates on the women's club ice hockey team sued after their fourth request for varsity status in nine years was denied. At Colorado State, the members of the softball team sued after their program was cancelled. Seven University of Texas female athletes got together and filed suit under Title IX on the sole ground that women were 47 percent of the students at Austin but only 23 percent of the athletic squads. And the California chapter of the National Organization for Women (Cal-NOW) sued the entire California State University system, charging that the state was failing to provide "equal opportunity" to female student-athletes because women were 55 percent of CSU students but only 30 percent of student-athletes.

In each of these cases, female athletes charged that *statistics*—not any invidious policy or hostile act on the part of the schools—proved they were victims of illegal discrimination. At each of the schools in question, the percentage of women in athletics didn't match the percentage of women in the student body as a whole, ergo the school must be biased against women. In much the same way that plaintiffs in racial discrimination cases had alleged bias because of a statistical "underrepresentation" of a particular minority group in a job, Title IX plaintiffs in the early 1990s charged that women who were "underrepresented" in athletics were victims of prima facie discrimination.

Ironically, while female athletes were using the courts to prove discrimination based on statistics, the courts were moving in the opposite direction in racial discrimination cases on the job. For example, in *Wards Cove v. Antonio* (1989) the Supreme Court ruled that statistics alone weren't enough to prove discrimination—or to force an employer into court to prove an absence of discrimination. Under *Wards Cove,* plaintiffs alleging racial discrimination in employment under the 1964 Civil Rights Act had to show disparate *treatment,* not just disparate *impact.* The plaintiffs had to prove that the employer's conduct was the cause of their group's underrepresentation at the company. And if the employer had a legitimate business reason for hiring certain people, he or she could not be sued for discrimination no matter what the numbers were. *Wards Cove* said that a federal bias case required some evidence of intentional discrimination, not simply an inference from statistics. The appropriate standard was innocent until proven guilty, and the burden was on the employees to prove the guilt of the employer, not on the employer to prove his or her innocence.

Title IX jurisprudence in the early 1990s, however, stood *Wards Cove* on its head. In these cases, the proportionality test took one glance at a school's statistical data, pronounced the school guilty on the basis of unbalanced numbers and forced it to prove itself innocent. Under this formulation, Title IX lawsuits were unqualified successes in the courts during that decade. With a single exception, the aggrieved female athletes and their supporters in the professional women's groups prevailed in every suit they brought. School after school either lost its case or settled out of court, on terms dictated by the plaintiffs and their attorneys.

Just two months after the lawsuit was filed against it, for instance, Auburn University agreed to make women's soccer a varsity sport. Colgate initially lost its women's ice hockey case, then won on appeal, and then settled out of court in a second lawsuit filed by a new group of athletes. After being found guilty of violating Title IX in courts, Colorado State agreed to reinstate its women's softball program. The University of Texas consented to bring its female athletic participation rate to within 3 percent of female enrollment.

In the most sweeping resolution of a sex discrimination lawsuit to that date, the California State University system similarly embraced gender quotas, agreeing to bring the percentage of women in athletics at each of its twenty institutions to within 5 percent of women's enrollment by 1998. Data from the fall of 1998 showed that on each of the CSU campuses except for Pomona, women were the majority of students. Under what is known as the CSU/Cal-NOW consent decree, women therefore must form the majority of athletes on each campus—even though surveys of current and prospective CSU students show that more men than women are interested in athletics. A poll taken of students enrolled in 1998–99 found that 61 percent of those interested in participating in intercollegiate athletics were men and 39 percent were women. A survey of prospective students uncovered a similar breakdown in athletic interest: 57 percent of men were interested versus 43 percent of women. Likewise, requests from current and prospective students for opportunities to compete in intercollegiate athletics came from men 57 percent of the time and women 43 percent of the time.[11]

As the Clinton administration and the courts were expanding

Title IX enforcement, the National Collegiate Athletics Association also got into the act. A 1991 NCAA survey of member institutions produced the large-scale statistical evidence that Title IX activists, both inside and outside the NCAA, had been waiting for: although enrollment was about evenly split between men and women at NCAA schools, 70 percent of athletes were men and (as Title IX requires) they received about 70 percent of scholarship dollars. NCAA executive director Dick Schultz quickly moved to declare "mere compliance" with the law insufficient. Although just years before, the NCAA had fought to exempt football from coverage under the law (so revenue-generating football squads wouldn't be cut in order to meet gender quotas), Schultz now proclaimed "gender equity" to be a "moral imperative." A task force was formed and charged with answering the question that virtually everyone agreed needed to be answered most: Just what was "gender equity"? How was it measured? And how would a college or university know it when it saw it?

THROUGHOUT HER CAREER AS the longest serving Office for Civil Rights chief in history, Norma Cantu relentlessly pursued an agenda built on the politics of gender and race, often in the face of contrary legal opinion from the courts. One of the more egregious examples of Cantu's zealotry involves race-based preferences, but nonetheless sheds important light on her determined crusade to create preferences for women under Title IX.

When Cheryl Hopwood was turned down by the University of Texas School of Law despite higher test scores than many minorities who were accepted, she sued. Her effort produced *Hopwood v. Texas,* in which the U.S. Court of Appeals for the Fifth Circuit struck down racial preferences in admissions not just to the University of Texas but to all colleges and universities under its jurisdiction. Following the ruling, Texas attorney general Dan Morales reluctantly set about implementing it. He advised Texas schools to dump dual-track admissions processes and put race-neutral policies in their place.

And then he ran into an unexpected roadblock. Norma Cantu wrote Morales to tell him he was wrong. In an opinion that flew in the face of all legal precedent, Cantu maintained that not only did *Hopwood* apply only to the University of Texas, but Texas schools that failed to retain or implement race-based admissions were in danger of losing their federal funding. Texans took Cantu's letter for the threat it was. Outraged senators threatened to withhold funding from the Education Department. Finally, after her own solicitor general contradicted her reading of *Hopwood,* Cantu backed down.

With equally glancing deference to the law, Cantu worked hard to pursue gender-based preferences. She collaborated opportunistically with groups outside her department to expand the meaning of Title IX. Although constrained from openly advocating a system of gender preferences by the unambiguous language of Title IX, Cantu engaged in a highly choreographed *pas de deux* with judges and women's groups who were free to advance the idea that Title IX guarantees not just equal opportunity but equal results. Changes in enforcement of the law that the OCR couldn't simply decree, it worked with courts to bring about by judicial interpretation. At other times Cantu issued informal policy "guidance" that stretched the meaning of the law. She bet (correctly) that colleges, universities, high schools and grade schools would take her "policy interpretations" for legally binding regulation.

Immediately upon taking office in 1993, Cantu convened a series of meetings with what one aide called "the usual stakeholders"— lawyers and women's groups—with the goal of strengthening OCR's enforcement of "gender equity" on campus. Said one former civil rights investigator for the OCR under Cantu: "They changed policy to accommodate the Women's Sports Foundation. The OCR became populated with zealots who had lost all objectivity. I knew something had changed when they began to refer to complainants as 'clients.'"

Cantu put both the NCAA and its member institutions on notice that the federal government backed the Title IX compliance regime that was evolving in the courts. "The courts have been very active," said Cantu deputy Jeannette Lim. "We want to reflect that."[12] As to the question of what constitutes "gender equity," Cantu was unambiguous. The NCAA's Gender Equity Task Force, she warned, should adopt the remedy of "proportionality" favored by the courts—or else. Speaking of the rigid quota imposed in the California NOW lawsuit, Cantu told the *New York Times,* "Cases such as this should have a significant effect on framing the discussions at the NCAA. They describe for the colleges the cost of continuing to have women underrepresented in intercollegiate athletics."[13]

But the "costs" of gender quotas under Title IX were being felt in more human ways, too. Suddenly forced to play an unyielding game of numbers, colleges and universities quickly mastered the zero-sum mathematics of gender equity: if they cut numbers from the men's side, the percentage of women rose automatically to meet the mandated proportion—without adding a single new opportunity for women.

In a cruel progression that would continue as the decade went on, men's teams at most of the schools involved in Title IX litigation in the early 1990s were cut in the name of increasing opportunities for women. The weakest were the first to go: the low-profile, so-called "nonrevenue" men's sports that can't match the drawing power, revenue generation and glamour of men's basketball and football. Colgate cut its 107-year-old men's baseball program. Colorado State also eliminated baseball. The University of Texas cut "walk-ons" to its men's teams—the nonscholarship athletes who come out only for the love of the game. And the twenty schools of the California State University system began to move painfully toward court-ordered "proportionality" by cutting baseball, men's volleyball, soccer and swimming at Cal State Northridge; football at Cal State Long Beach, Cal State Fullerton and Cal State San Francisco; and men's cross-country at Cal State San Diego. The wrestling program at Cal State Bakersfield even went coed in an effort to add female participants and save itself from elimination under Title IX.

The question of just what constituted "gender equity" in college athletics, it seemed, was answered. For Title IX activists, what remained was to make sure that the new standard was strictly enforced in America's colleges, universities and high schools.

THE CUTS TO MEN'S SPORTS TEAMS that accelerated in the 1990s in the name of gender equity produced many victims. These victims were dismissed—and the injustice of the new Title IX regime overlooked—because of the assumption that the law had liberated into sports a generation of women who would not otherwise have had the opportunity to compete. But this ends-justifies-the-means argument is flawed on two counts. First, it is certainly open to debate whether the end (more teams for women) in fact justifies the means (fewer teams for men). Second, it is far from proven that Title IX was responsible for the end to begin with.

Author and social scientist Charles Murray has written about the difficulties inherent in trying to prove that a particular government action produced—or failed to produce—a particular result. The bottom line, according to Murray, is that "proof" is unattainable because government policy is only one of a virtually infinite set of variables that combine to produce a given outcome. Isolating that policy from broader social and economic trends is impossible.

This is perhaps true of no government policy more than Title IX. Those who argue that the championship Women's World Cup soccer team would never have come about without a federal law prohibiting sex discrimination can no more "prove" their proposition than can those who contend the opposite, that the changed social circumstances of the 1960s and 1970s would have been sufficient to produce a world champion women's team without government action. Still, there are things we know that strongly suggest that the connection between the enactment of Title IX and the advent of the world championship women's soccer team is considerably less direct than women's groups maintain.

Title IX was enacted in 1972 at a time when the "revolution" in women's sports had already begun and girls and women were enthusiastically taking to the basketball courts and softball fields of the nation's schools. At that stage of its legislative development, Title IX was far from the preference regime it would later become. It was primarily a powerful symbolic statement of a principle that was already being honored voluntarily by growing numbers of schools in the 1970s. There were holdouts to be sure, but as more and more girls and women demanded the opportunity to compete in athletics, more and more institutions complied—without a federal enforcement bureaucracy looking over their shoulders. It took the federal government to codify the principle that the people's money would not be used to deny girls and women access to the playing field. But only the people themselves could create the social environment that led girls and women to seek such access to begin with.

Charles Murray tests the efficacy of government programs in bringing about social change with what he calls the "trendline test." This is precisely what it sounds like: the trendline test examines a behavioral trend before and after the enactment of a new government policy to see how, or if, behavior changes in response to that policy. For instance, Murray shows that deaths from motor vehicle accidents—widely reported to have been reduced by government imposition of the 55-mile-an-hour speed limit in 1974—actually began to decline in 1925 and had their steepest drop-off between 1934 and 1949.[14]

The trendline test is just the first stop in analyzing a government policy, not the last. Murray points out that myriad other variables are involved in generating a particular social outcome. Measuring the effects of a government program designed to increase employment, for example, would be complicated by the onset of a recession the year it was enacted. Nonetheless, the trendline test can help answer a threshold question about the impact of Title IX: is there any evidence that the law caused an increase in the athletic participation of American girls and women?

The favorite factoid of defenders of Title IX quotas who contend that Title IX is responsible for women's gains in sports is this:

> *Before Title IX, 1 in 27 high school girls played sports. Today, that number is 1 in 3.*

This statistic is true, and it represents a gain for young women of which all Americans can and should be proud. But it is also beguiling: under the guise of saying something profound about cause and effect, it actually only offers two snapshots in time of women's participation in sports. In fact, when Title IX is subjected to the more dynamic analysis of the trendline test, we see that girls and women began to increase their participation in sports significantly *before* the law was passed. What's more, the greatest athletic gains of girls and women occurred before implementing regulations existed to enforce Title IX in the nation's schools.

Unfortunately, the earliest that statistics were recorded on girls' participation in high school sports was 1971, which gives us only one year of data before the passage of the law. But even this limited look shows strong movement by girls onto the athletic field before Congress codified their right to do so in 1972. Between 1971 and 1972, the number of girls playing high school sports jumped almost threefold, from 294,015 to 817,073.[15] The formulation favored by Title IX quota defenders should therefore be modified in this way:

> *In 1971, 1 in 27 high school girls played sports. In 1972, the year Title IX was passed, 1 in 9 girls played sports. Today, that number is 1 in 3.*

This is an altogether different story from the one feminists tell. The momentum with which young female athletes were entering high school sports between 1971 and 1972 tells us that this was a trend that did not originate with the passage of Title IX but began years earlier. Did the publicity and debate surrounding passage of Title IX encourage and support this momentum? Almost certainly it did. But did Title IX initiate this movement? Clearly not.

"Something very important happened to change the participation of girls in high school athletics. You had to have a major shift in the trendline somewhere in the late Sixties or early Seventies," says Murray. "Athletic participation of girls really did change and that change occurred before 1972. By the time the law was passed, that fundamental shift was already in motion."

But what about the years after 1972? If Title IX didn't start the women's revolution in sports, didn't it at least provide the legal club that beat recalcitrant schools and athletic departments into line? Here again the trendline test can't tell the whole story but it can offer some important clues.

As we have seen, regulations implementing Title IX in sports weren't published until 1979 with the Athletics Policy Interpretation. This meant that for most of the decade of the 1970s, although Title IX stood on the books as a powerful symbol of the nation's commitment to nondiscrimination on the basis of sex, the law was unenforced and unenforceable in sporting programs in the nation's schools.

And yet, as the graph below shows, the steepest point in the upward trajectory of high school girls' athletic participation in the past thirty years occurs in the Seventies—before Title IX was being implemented in athletics. By the time the Carter administration Department of Heath, Education and Welfare published its "interpretation" in December 1979, almost one in four high school girls played sports. In less than a decade, the number of female high school athletes had risen almost 600 percent. It would take another two decades for that number to climb another 50 percent.

High School Female Athletic Participation

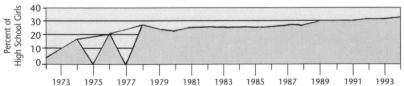

Since the passage of Title IX, increases in sports participation among college women have been similarly dramatic. But here again, the gains began before 1972 and were greatest in the late 1960s, 1970s and early 1980s. According to the NCAA, the number of women playing intercollegiate sports doubled in the five years before Title IX (1966 to 1971), from around 15,000 to just over 30,000. Granted, this number represented a small fraction of all women in colleges and universities—about 1.7 percent of all full-time female undergraduates in 1971. But clearly something was causing college women to begin to turn out for organized sports. By the mid-Seventies, 3.1 percent of all coeds were varsity athletes, a number that peaked at 5.5 percent in the mid-1980s.[16]

Since the mid-Eighties, girls and women in athletics have continued to gain, but at much lower rates than before. In a study prepared for Representative Patsy Mink, a Hawaii Democrat and a strong Title IX supporter, the government General Accounting Office (GAO) reported that since the mid-Eighties, although the numbers of college-age female athletes and college women's teams have continued to rise, those increases have been just slightly ahead of the increase in enrollment of women as full-time undergraduates. Only today have female student-athletes regained the high-water mark set in 1986 of 5.5 percent of all female full-time undergraduates, or 157,000 athletes.[17] In high schools, girls' participation in athletics has also made slow, steady gains. From just under a third in 1986, the rate of participation of high school girls has slowly inched its way up to around 36 percent today.

But participation rates tell only a tiny fraction of the tangled story of Title IX and female athletes in the past three decades:

- *Fact:* NCAA member colleges and universities sponsor more athletic programs for women than for men—553 more, to be precise.
- *Fact:* The average female student-athlete now receives more scholarship aid than the average male student-athlete. A GAO study of 532 of the 596 NCAA institutions that grant athletic scholarships showed that these schools spent $4,458 in scholarships per male athlete and $4,861 per female athlete.
- *Fact:* Title IX implementing regulations require that the amount of scholarship aid given by a school mirror the gender balance of the school's athletes. Based on this requirement, over half of NCAA Division II and III colleges and universities now find

themselves in violation of Title IX for giving *too much* financial assistance to female athletes vis-à-vis male athletes.

IF WOMEN IN COLLEGES AND universities today have more athletic teams to choose from than men, and receive more athletic scholarship aid per capita than men, where are all the claims of "gender inequity" coming from? In what way are American schools falling short of their obligation under the law to provide equal opportunity to girls and women?

The answer, as usual, is in the numbers. The Department of Education's Office for Civil Rights uses what it calls a "three-part test"—first introduced in the 1979 Athletics Policy Interpretation—to measure compliance in athletic participation under Title IX. Officials at the OCR insist that the three-part test is progressive; compliance, they say, is measured in stages. If a school is unable to comply under the first test, it may do so under the second and, failing there, it has a final opportunity under the third test. In any case, a school need pass only one of the three tests to be in compliance with the law, so federal officials say.

The first and most important part of the three-part test, or "prong one" as Title IX aficionados like to call it, is proportionality itself. Under this test, federal investigators make a threshold determination of a school's compliance with Title IX by asking whether "opportunities for male and female students are provided in numbers substantially proportionate to their respective enrollments." The Office for Civil Rights has never explicitly defined what "substantial proportionality" means, although the courts have generally settled on an athletics participation rate that is within plus or minus 5 percent of the sex ratio of the student body.

Critics like Harvard Medical School ethics lecturer Louis M. Guenin point out that "prong one" employs a logical fallacy in establishing a benchmark determination of whether or not a school is in compliance with Title IX. Here's how it works:

The proportionality test begins by concluding, reasonably enough, that inequality between the sexes must be present where there is discrimination against girls and women. No problem here. We know that back when colleges and universities actively discriminated against females by limiting the number of women in their student bodies and on their athletic teams, girls' and women's participation in higher education and in athletics suffered in comparison with that of boys and men. But where the authors of the three-part test went wrong was in taking this logical conclusion and going a step further, into illogic: If participation is unequal when there is discrimination, they concluded, *then whenever there is unequal participation there must be discrimination.*

This test of "fairness" rests not on how many teams a school offers women, or even how many athletic scholarship dollars they receive. In the "boys versus girls" mentality of Title IX activists, the most important issue is how athletic participation and resources are divided between the sexes. *How many women are athletes as a percentage of all athletes; and does that percentage match the number of women in the school itself?* It matters not a whit if the school has a hundred athletes, a thousand athletes or no athletes at all, as long as roughly 50 percent of them are female. If they are, the school is judged to be in compliance with Title IX and federal investigators look no further. If not, and women are the "underrepresented sex" in its athletics program, the school is presumed to be discriminating and has the burden of establishing its innocence under the remaining two parts of the three-part test.

The second part asks if a school in which women are the "underrepresented sex" can nonetheless "show a history and continuing practice of program expansion" for women. Belmont University in Nashville, Tennessee, for example, was judged by OCR to be in compliance with the law in 1998 even though it didn't meet the proportionality test because it was in the process of adding three new women's teams. But the problem with "prong two" is that it doesn't specify an endpoint. How much "continuous program expansion" for women is enough? The logical answer, of course, is when women are no longer "underrepresented." That is, when the school has reached proportionality as defined by "prong one."

Finally, a school that is neither proportional under prong one nor moving toward proportionality under prong two has a last chance of proving its innocence by "demonstrat[ing] that the interests and abilities of [the underrepresented sex] have been fully and effectively accommodated by the present program." In theory at least, "prong three" offers an easy out: schools can offer more athletic opportunities to men than women and still be in compliance with the law as long as these unequal offerings aren't the result of discrimination.

In practice, however, prong three offers the least protection for a school seeking to prove nondiscrimination under Title IX. OCR has offered only limited guidance to schools attempting to meet this test, suggesting that requests by students to add sports, participation in intramural and club sports, surveys of students and even sports offered at surrounding high schools will be used to determine whether there is unmet interest on campus. And here, again, no endpoint is defined. What does it mean to "fully and effectively accommodate" women's interest in sports? Does this test obligate a university to offer an athletic team to every woman who comes along and requests one? The vagueness of the standard, as well as the time and expense involved in proving it in court or to federal investigators, offers little appeal to schools seeking a "safe harbor" of compliance under Title IX.

So the three-part test is regressive, not progressive; it stands the American legal tradition of "innocent until proven guilty" on its head. The first test, proportionality, establishes the guilt or innocence of the school in question. If the school meets the statistical test, it is off the hook. If it doesn't, it has two other tests by which to prove its innocence. But as we've seen, the second test is really just a way station to the first, and the third is vague and unreliable.

In fact, say critics of the law, the three-part test of Title IX compliance is actually a one-part test: statistical proportionality. "The law, despite claims to the contrary, does not allow for the possibility of differing levels of interest in sports. It just does not," says Leo Kocher, head wrestling coach at the University of Chicago. He offers an illuminating example:

> Say there's a school that has equal numbers of boys and girls and it decides to offer 200 athletic opportunities. If they have 100 girls who say they want to play sports and they have 1,000 boys who say they want to play sports, the law says that you must give 100 opportunities to those 100 girls and you must give 100 opportunities to those 1,000 boys. In the end, 100 percent of the girls are fully accommodated but only 10 percent of the boys are taken care of.

OCR OFFICIALS MAINTAIN THAT they judiciously leave it to the schools themselves to determine how they will comply with Title IX. In the majority of cases, they say, schools choose—of their own free will—one of the two nonquota methods to comply with the law: either expanding women's teams or accommodating the interests of women in sports.

"I think it's disingenuous to say that Title IX is a good law but that it's poorly regulated. It implies that the enforcement agency is trying to do damage to the children of America," complained Mary Francis O'Shea, national coordinator for athletics in the Clinton administration OCR, in response to criticism from coaches. "I can tell you as a matter of fact that schools have used all three parts of the compliance test."[18] O'Shea claims that about a third of the schools forced into Title IX compliance agreements with OCR between 1992 and 1999 chose proportionality as the way to shield themselves from federal action or lawsuits, while two-thirds chose the nonquota methods of compliance.

An analysis of cases resolved by the Clinton OCR reveals O'Shea's contention as a very narrowly crafted technical truth disguising a deeper lie. A Freedom of Information Act request of Title IX compliance agreements between the OCR and colleges and universities from 1992 to 2000 produced a much smaller number of athletics participation cases than O'Shea claims were handled by the OCR during the Clinton years (44 versus O'Shea's number of 116). Still, the agreements that specified a means of compliance in this smaller universe of cases broke down in roughly the same way she described: 11 schools, or 25 percent, agreed to Title IX compliance through proportionality (half of these schools explicitly agreeing in writing with OCR to cut men's opportunities); only 5 schools, or 8 percent, agreed to continue expanding women's teams; and 28 schools, around 64 percent of the total, chose "prong three," accommodating the interests and abilities of women on campus.

What these statistics fail to show is that in only three cases of all those handled by the Clinton OCR did the agency investigate a school, find that it had not yet reached proportionality, *and still declare that it was in compliance with the law*. What's more, in these three cases, colleges and universities were pronounced "innocent" under the second part of the three-part test only because they were in the process of adding multiple women's teams. In the overwhelming majority of cases in which schools chose the third option of meeting the interests of female students in sports, these schools were also forced to commit in writing to OCR to add women's teams. In other words, for the OCR it had nothing to do with the uniqueness of the school, its student body or their desires. It was only a game of numbers.

BUT WHAT ABOUT THE ASSERTION that began this chapter: What is the evidence that Title IX "produced" the most high-profile women's athletic success story to date, the 1999 Women's World Cup soccer team?

As it was for most of their sisters in athletics, most of the members of the U.S. women's soccer team took their first steps into the playing field during the transformational decade of the 1970s, a decade in which Title IX was on the books but lacked the daunting superstructure of implementation that it would acquire over the next thirty years. And even for most of the 1980s, when seven of the eleven starters on the women's team joined the national squad as teenagers, Title IX was literally inoperative in the nation's schools due to the Supreme Court's *Grove City v. Bell* ruling, which exempted athletics from coverage under Title IX.* It wasn't until the early 1990s, when Clinton administration civil rights enforcers began to work with women's groups and activist courts to change the meaning of the law, that Title IX began to be actively enforced in the nation's schools. By then it was too late to have made the difference for the women of World Cup soccer; they had already begun to win international championships without the aid of a federal law.

It is true that girls' and women's soccer programs have exploded in American educational institutions in the years since Title IX was passed. But it is also true that the formative soccer experience of the women's national team—like that of millions of American girls—was not in school-sponsored play under rigid rules about gender equity but in independent youth leagues. Here, outside the jurisdiction of Title IX, competition for young girls has proliferated in the past quarter-century with a governance comprised not of federal bureaucrats but of moms and dads who shuttle pigtailed players to and from practice in minivans.

The ritualistic attribution of the success of the U.S. women's soccer team—and by extension all successful female athletes—to Title IX

---

*Under Attorney General Ed Meese, the Reagan administration sided with Grove City College, a small Pennsylvania school outside of Pittsburgh that was challenging the scope of federal civil rights laws whose mandate attached to the acceptance of federal monies. Grove City argued that because it didn't receive any direct federal funding—only indirect funding through federal student loans and grants—it shouldn't be bound by Title IX and Title VI of the Civil Rights Act. The Reagan administration, Meese announced, agreed, and the Supreme Court granted Grove City College a limited victory in 1984. Instead of freeing the entire institution from the grip of federal regulation under Title VI and Title IX, the high court ruled that only those educational programs within the school that received direct federal aid would be bound by civil rights laws. At Grove City, that meant only the financial aid office had to worry about Title IX compliance. In 1988, Congress passed the Civil Rights Restoration Act, reversing the *Grove City* decision and once again extending Title IX's application to all aspects of institutions that receive federal funds.

oversimplifies complex social changes in America that produced equal opportunity for women, and it also demeans talented athletes and their accomplishments. When was the first (and last) time the network news attributed the success of Hewlett-Packard CEO Carly Fiorina to the federal law barring discrimination in employment? Or, for that matter, when has the *New York Times* reported that the 1965 Voting Rights Act is "responsible" for the careers of African-American politicians like Charlie Rangel, Maxine Waters and John Conyers?

The linkage of successful female athletes with Title IX relies for its credibility on the assumption that American schools, particularly colleges and universities, are patriarchal throwbacks to the era when girls played basketball half-court and their softball uniforms were skirts. Any gains made by women, so this theory goes, must have been wrenched forcibly by the federal government from the beefy hands of the white, heterosexual men who controlled these institutions for centuries. In fact, this parable of victimization is a cartoon. The American academy has gone to great, often quite ridiculous lengths to be open and accommodating to women; witness the fact that women are now a majority of undergraduates and degree earners.

That the obligatory linking of the U.S. women's soccer team and Title IX is more a political assertion than a historical truth is shown by the fact that the American women were winning long before the summer of 1999—and nobody bothered to say it was because of Title IX. As editorial writer David Tell has noted, in 1991 the U.S. women demolished the Norwegian national team to win the first-ever Women's World Cup soccer championship. But no one—not a single sports writer, editorial writer, politician or spokesperson for a women's group—laid their victory at the feet of a federal law.

What was different in 1999 was the political setting. The World Cup championship was being played in America, guaranteeing maximum media coverage. In addition, there was a felt need on the part of advocates in 1999 to defend Title IX after media reports of cuts to men's teams—some from surprising sources like CBS's *60 Minutes* and ABC's *20/20*—had begun to surface. Women's soccer put a positive face on what some were beginning to understand was a law with a significant downside.

It was a strategy that Title IX feminists had successfully pursued before. At each landmark in the advance of women's athletics, they had worked with cowed corporations and a compliant news media to attribute women's success to Title IX. During the 1996 Olympics,

Nike, the athletic footwear giant, aired a commercial in which a narrator read directly from the text of Title IX over still photos of winning female athletes. The 1997 launch of the Women's National Basketball Association (WNBA) was portrayed as a parable of the power of Title IX. At opening games, stadiums were festooned with banners declaring "Thanks Title IX!" And women's groups worked with Nike, Reebok and other athletic gear manufacturers to sponsor media campaigns and publicity materials spreading the good news of "gender equity."

What feminists and their allies saw in Mia Hamm and Brandi Chastain in the summer of 1999 was the opportunity to take their campaign to a new level. With the active collaboration of the Clinton administration and the courts, they had succeeded in making "proportionality" the reigning standard of Title IX compliance, and the tremendous success of Women's World Cup soccer was proof of that success. Now, new areas of education were opening up in which Title IX could be used to force preferences for girls and women.

One broad, new frontier for Title IX feminists had opened in March 1999 when the Supreme Court held that school districts could be held liable for damages resulting from student-on-student sexual harassment. Title IX had for many years formed the basis of lawsuits brought by parents who felt their daughters or sons had been harassed by teachers and administrators, but now the court was saying that the law covered sexual harassment by fellow students as well. It was a breathtaking expansion of liability for schools. What was once normal playground teasing between little boys and little girls was suddenly a potential lawsuit for school districts. Behavior that had previously been dealt with through normal disciplinary action was now suddenly infused with the heat and uncertainty of gender politics. Schools were forced to take needed resources from school safety and drug prevention programs and devote them to student sexual harassment training and procedures in order to shield themselves from liability.

But perhaps the greatest potential expansion of Title IX came in the summer of 1999 with the "unified rule" that the Clinton administration was developing to take Title IX enforcement from the exclusive purview of the Education Department's Office for Civil Rights and extend it to the entire federal bureaucracy. Twenty-nine federal agencies and departments, including every cabinet-level department, dispensed federal money used for educational purposes. Clinton officials in the Department of Justice declared that these departments too would be charged with seeing that such funds were used in accordance with their definition of "gender equity." The federal government was preparing not simply to step up Title IX enforcement, said one Clinton Justice Department official, but to "begin" it.

This offensive is what feminists wanted most to protect when they launched their successful campaign to claim the victory of the U.S. women's soccer team for Title IX. After this coup, the entire world of education was their oyster. Why should Title IX be limited to athletics? The National Science Foundation gives out more than $100 million to undergraduate science, engineering and mathematics programs each year; why not demand "gender equity" here as well? The Department of Health and Human Services doles out tens of millions of dollars for training nurses each year; why not use the law to see that at least half of these nurses are men? Quota advocates had "won the sports battle," said Michael Williams, former OCR head in the Bush administration. Now their sights were set on the vast expanse of federally funded education off the playing field.

It was the revenge of the Equal Rights Amendment. In the aftermath of that crushing defeat, some feminists had the prescience to see another way to realize the agenda of the ERA: through federal laws like Title IX. It wasn't as sexy. It would take longer and cost more. But in the end, it could achieve the same benefits for women in a huge swath of American life.

The women's movement has changed much since 1972, when Congress passed Title IX along with the ERA; and Title IX has changed with it. Passed in the spirit of respect for women despite their differences from men, the law now embodies the same principle of government-enforced androgyny that informed the ERA—the belief that men and women are undifferentiated in their abilities and inclinations; that any disparity in behavior or performance necessarily results from discrimination or the legacy of centuries of past discrimination; and that because so many activities do in fact yield such disparities, the federal government must step in to erase them.

These notions were rejected by two-thirds of the state legislatures when they voted down the ERA. But Title IX achieves this vision of a radically different America by other means.

TWO

A FIELD OF NIGHTMARES

*Lisa, if the Bible has taught us nothing else—and it
hasn't—it's that girls should stick to girls' sports, such
as hot-oil wrestling and foxy boxing and such and such.*
— Homer Simpson

MIKE SCOTT CAME TO Providence College in Rhode Island for
one reason: to play baseball. His dad had played college
ball, spent some time in the minors and was now a high
school baseball coach. The younger Scott had been playing baseball
since he was old enough to hold a bat. Now he had his eye on a
chance at the big time: to play in the majors.

Providence, Mike thought, was the place to begin his journey.
Since joining the program as an assistant coach in 1991, head coach
Charlie Hickey had worked to build the eighty-year-old Friars program into a Northeast powerhouse. In the 1990s, the team began to
attract NCAA tournament bids and recorded just one losing season.
And although it was college baseball in New England, where players
roughed out the cold spring seasons for the sheer love of the game,
Providence began to attract high-quality recruits like Mike Scott. "We
were beginning to threaten Northeast powerhouses like Seton Hall
and St. Johns," says Hickey. "We had what I think what most people in New England consider one of the elite programs."

Recruited as a standout high school hitter, Scott briefly considered
the baseball program at the University of New Hampshire. But when
UNH announced that it was cutting baseball in order to comply with
Title IX, he turned to Providence College. And although Coach
Hickey couldn't offer him a scholarship, only a spot on the team
and a chance to play, that was enough. Scott entered Providence in
1997, was injured and had to sit out his freshman season. Then, one
crisp fall day in October 1998, just two weeks into the pre-season
practice schedule of Scott's sophomore year, Coach Hickey was

summoned from the practice field into Providence athletic director John Marinatto's office. A few minutes later, he returned to the practice diamond to present Scott and his teammates with shocking news: the 1998–99 baseball season would be the Friars' last.

The reason was Title IX. Because Providence—like virtually every college and university—receives some federal money in some form, the school was legally bound to comply with the provisions of the law.

But Scott and his teammates were confused: what women had faced discrimination at Providence? The Catholic university had a strong program of athletics for females. Of the twenty varsity programs carried by the college, half were for women, including the latest hot women's intercollegiate sport, ice hockey. No female athlete had filed a complaint of discrimination at Providence, and no investigation had found a pattern of discrimination that somehow had escaped complaint. What, Scott and his teammates wondered, was wrong at Providence College?

The answer could be found in a set of statistics that Marinatto had compiled that fall and submitted to the Department of Education in Washington, D.C. The Equity in Athletics Disclosure Act (EADA) requires that all colleges and universities submit a mind-boggling array of detailed information on their sports programs, broken down by sex. Schools report the number of athletic participants by sex, the assignment of head coaches by sex, operating expenses by sex, recruitment expenses by sex, coaches' salaries by sex, and on and on. In addition, the EADA demands one statistic that has nothing to do with athletics: schools must compile and submit the number of full-time undergraduates, by sex.

Feminist women's groups like the American Association of University Women pushed hard for passage of the EADA—with data on the gender balance of the student body included—in order to expedite the process of bringing lawsuits against schools under Title IX. By framing the issue in terms of "equity" they were able to convince Congress to impose yet another bookkeeping burden on colleges and universities, and create a taxpayer-funded database with which to pursue Title IX "proportionality." Previously, finding the data needed to bring a lawsuit under Title IX necessitated a little digging; but the EADA created a readymade client shopping list for trial lawyers. One glance at a school's EADA submission shows a would-be plaintiff's attorney whether or not a school is vulnerable to a Title IX lawsuit.

When Providence College filled out its EADA form in the fall of

1998, the findings set off alarm bells in the administration. Like the majority of colleges and universities today, Providence's student body was majority female, and growing more so, but its athletic program had failed to keep pace. Drawn by the security of Providence's Catholic tradition, women comprised a whopping 59 percent of all students in the fall of 1998. Female student-athletes, however, were only 48 percent of all varsity athletes. This was well above the national average of 40 percent female athletic participation, but not enough to pass the Title IX "proportionality" test. Adding enough women's teams to meet proportionality, Providence's Gender Equity Compliance Committee calculated, would cost $3 million, a prohibitive expense for the school. Providence had "too many" male athletes—11 percent too many, to be exact. Something had to give.

Seven years earlier, Providence's cross-town rival, Brown University, was sued by a group of female athletes when it attempted to de-fund two men's and two women's varsity teams in a cost-saving effort. The female athletes at Brown argued that cutting women's teams was illegal under Title IX because the university had not yet achieved proportionality—despite offering more teams for women than any other school in the country except Harvard. Brown decided to fight the lawsuit, arguing that Title IX required it to provide women equal opportunity to participate in athletics, not guarantee that they actually participate at the same rate as men. A series of adverse rulings led Brown all the way to the Supreme Court, which declined to hear the case. The result was that the rulings of the lower courts stood: Title IX was interpreted to mean that the university did, in fact, have an obligation to see that women participated in sports as enthusiastically as men. The case (which will be explored in more detail later) was a landmark in the institutionalization of quotas under Title IX. Colleges and universities across the country began to cut men's teams to comply with what the Court had decreed was the correct interpretation of the law.

Mindful of Brown's experience, Providence College did what all colleges and universities are today increasingly forced to do: consult its lawyers. Their advice was direct: the only way for Providence to insulate itself from a Title IX lawsuit or federal investigation was somehow to add enough female athletes, or subtract enough male athletes, to close the gap. So instead of imposing double-digit tuition increases to raise the funds for new women's teams, Providence chose to boost the number of its women athletes artificially by subtracting from the men's side of the sports ledger.

"They were looking for three things," says Coach Hickey. "They were looking for which sports had the number of participants to cut to bring them closer to proportionality, which sports had the scholarships they could transfer to the women's side, and which sports had the operating budget they could save money on."

Providence baseball had it all: twenty-eight bodies on the playing field, seven scholarships split among them and $380,000 in operating expenses. Coach Hickey implored the Providence administration to save baseball by allowing the program to raise the necessary funds itself. He was informed that if such a dispensation were granted, Providence baseball would also have to raise enough funds to cover the creation of one or more women's teams necessary to "compensate" for retaining twenty-eight male athletes. "We were originally told, go ahead and raise the $380,000 but on top of that you have to raise 59 percent more," says Hickey. "We're talking about having to come up with $750,000 every year, just to guarantee to play." In the end, the only feasible solution was to cut, not add. By eliminating baseball, men's golf and men's tennis and capping the number of men who competed on the remaining eight men's programs, Providence achieved "proportionality." Without the addition of a single women's athletic opportunity, the percentage of female athletes rose from 47 percent to 57 percent.

Suddenly, a season that had begun so hopefully for Mike Scott and Charlie Hickey took on even more importance. Determined to go out with a bang, not a whimper, Scott and his teammates redoubled their efforts on the playing field. Second baseman Paul Costello recalled a line from *Major League,* a movie about a faltering group of professional baseball players: "There's only one thing left to do: Win the whole #$%&* thing!" The team adopted it as their unofficial motto. "We wanted to make a statement," says Scott, "and that was perfect."

And Providence baseball did indeed go on to win the whole thing. The 1998–99 season was the most successful in the school's history. Scott's team won forty-three games in the regular season and then four more to capture the Big East championship. With Mike Scott setting the pace, they led the nation in hits and were ranked twenty-first in the country. At the NCAA regional championship tournament in Tallahassee, the Friars took on Florida State, ranked second nationally, to conclude their season. "We played like there was no tomorrow because there literally was no tomorrow," says Hickey. But in the end, it didn't matter. Rev. Philip A. Smith, president of Providence College, skipped the last home game. The Friars lost to Florida State, and Scott and his teammates decided not to turn in their uniforms.

FEMINISTS CALL THE STRUGGLE FOR proportionality under Title IX the pursuit of "gender equity." The Women's Sports Foundation (WSF) is perhaps the strongest advocate of Title IX and "gender equity" in sports, having as its mission to "increase and enhance sports and fitness opportunities for all girls and women."

Founded by tennis player Billie Jean King in 1974 in the afterglow of her victory over Bobby Riggs in the "Battle of the Sexes," the WSF is the most powerful advocacy group for female athletes in the country. Like most women's groups, it has benefited from friendly press coverage. But unlike most women's groups, the WSF has made genuine heroes its public face: women like Mia Hamm, Julie Foudy and Michelle Akers of the championship U.S. Women's World Cup soccer team, Kym Hampton and Rebecca Lobo of the Women's National Basketball Association, two-time heptathlon winner Jackie Joyner-Kersee, sprinter Gail Devers, swimmer Summer Sanders and gold-medal-winning gymnast Dominique Moceanu. This strategy of capitalizing on the popularity of female athletes has made the WSF a magnet for corporate giving. General Motors and Merrill Lynch are generous supporters. Representatives of Reebok, Mervyn's of California and the Sporting Goods Manufacturers Association sit on its board of trustees. Their support allows the WSF to rake in additional contributions at a glittering gala each year in New York City and dole out more than $1 million a year in grants and scholarships to female athletes.

But behind the appealing image of strong female athleticism that is the group's public face, the Women's Sports Foundation pursues a relentlessly political agenda: to turn the grant of opportunity for women guaranteed under Title IX into a grant of preference. Under the leadership of its street-fighting executive director, Donna Lopiano, a former All-American softball player and the former women's athletic director at the University of Texas, the WSF has done more than any other group to convince colleges and universities that compliance with Title IX means manipulating the numbers of male and female athletes.

Lopiano, who calls those who disagree with her version of equity "dinosaurs," came to the WSF in 1992 fresh from Austin, where she was instrumental in fomenting a landmark Title IX lawsuit against her own university for its failure to achieve proportionality. Lopiano was the first to admit that Texas wasn't guilty of any bias against women, only of failing to give them the preferences she believes they deserve. "Texas did a better job with women's athletics than anybody in the country," she said after the lawsuit had been filed. "Did they make their best effort? Yes. Did they comply with federal law? No."[1]

The Texas case was a landmark because up to that point, court victories won by female athletes to create Title IX quotas had been limited to mandating the reinstatement of teams that had been cut. The Lopiano-inspired Texas case, in contrast, demanded that women's teams be *added* to fill the gender quota. Thanks to revenues brought in by Longhorn football, Texas had a bigger women's athletic budget than any other two schools in its conference combined. Still, female athletic participation—the responsibility of the recently departed Lopiano—was stuck at around 23 percent in the early 1990s. So even though the administration was already in the process of adding two women's sports, it settled before the case got to court, agreeing to reach proportionality by the 1995–96 academic year. Additional women's teams were added while nonscholarship male athletes—who, by outnumbering female nonscholarship athletes 81 to 1, accounted for much of Texas's "Title IX gap"—were cut.

Lopiano brought the same passion for gender engineering to the Women's Sports Foundation. Her strategy, she told reporters in 1992, was to "break the bank," forcing schools to spend so much to meet the gender quota that what she regarded as the corrupt, male-dominated edifice of collegiate sports would fall entirely and be replaced by "gender equity." And if schools wouldn't spend on athletics, Lopiano made sure they spent on litigation. Moreover, according to former OCR investigator Lamar Daniel, she is credited with "taking over" the NCAA Gender Equity Task Force that declared proportionality the "ultimate goal" of member institutions in 1993—a requirement that has led to regular "gender equity" certification of schools by the NCAA.

In addition, under Lopiano the WSF has worked tirelessly to cultivate future litigants and future complainants in Title IX cases. It maintains an "Equity Hotline" complete with a staff ready to help with attorney referrals, and "how-to" literature and expert assistance on everything from the rights of local girls' softball leagues to the arcana of federal regulations. There is an online database that ranks schools according to their commitment to gender equity and allows users to automatically share that ranking with local media and state and federal politicians. To keep Congress and the media aware of its efforts, the WSF sponsors National Girls and Women in Sports Day. Events are staged across the country and female athletes flood their congressperson's and senator's offices to remind them of the importance of gender equity in athletics.

But the Women's Sports Foundation, however formidable, is only one part of a coalition of liberal women's groups, trial lawyers and "gender equity" advocates and consultants for whom Title IX is the *sine qua non* of existence. The American Association of University Women (AAUW) focuses on Title IX issues outside sports. And the National Women's Law Center (NWLC), another major player in the battle for gender equity, provides critical legal support.

Any attempt to change Title IX enforcement, even in a small way, will meet with great resistance from these groups. "The law means everything," says Donna deVarona, former Olympic swimming champ and WSF founding member. "Sports is the most visible affirmation of what Title IX did. But if you look behind it—if you look at the success of women in business, the success of women as lawyers, as leaders and, hopefully, as politicians—our very lifeblood depends on Title IX."

AT JAMES MADISON UNIVERSITY, as at the majority of universities, women were a rising majority of the student body in 2000 but a lagging minority of athletes, even though JMU offered its women more athletic teams than most schools—and more than it offered its men. Lady Dukes ran track and cross-country, and played basketball, volleyball, tennis, soccer, lacrosse, golf and field hockey. They even shot archery, fenced and swam. What they didn't do was engage in these team activities at the same rate as JMU men. The result was that in the 2000–01 school year, females were 58 percent of the James Madison student body but only 41 percent of student-athletes.

James Madison was failing prong one of the three-part test and Al Taliaferro knew it. So on April 2, 2000, Taliaferro, the father of a senior on the JMU women's club softball team, wrote the Department of Education's Office for Civil Rights to complain. Despite earlier assurances from university officials, Taliaferro wrote, JMU had not upgraded his daughter's softball team from partially funded club status to university-funded varsity status. Using JMU's Equity in Athletics Disclosure (EADA) form documenting JMU's 17-point "Title IX gap" as his resource, Taliaferro contended that the refusal to upgrade his daughter's team, given the disparity of participation in women's and men's athletics at JMU, was illegal under federal law.

"James Madison has blatantly discriminated in violation of Title IX on the basis of sex against female athletes for many years," he wrote. The university, he demanded, must create a varsity softball team "immediately, without further delay." Either that, Taliaferro insisted, or "the college should be forced to eliminate its baseball program until it can provide equity to both programs."

The three-part test forced James Madison officials to take Taliaferro's remarks seriously. At minimum, his complaint would trigger a lengthy, expensive investigation by federal officials that was likely to come out badly for JMU. At maximum, the school could lose its federal funding. The officials wanted to do the right thing, but they couldn't afford to increase the size of their women's sports program. While other schools in their conference offered an average of 18 teams, JMU featured a whopping 27. Given this already full sports offering, showing a "continuing process of program expansion" for women under prong two was out of the question.

Administrators reached out to a "gender equity" consultant for guidance on what to do. The consultant, a veteran of two decades of service in the Office for Civil Rights, advised them that the final test, prong three, offered little protection. As long as the university had failed to achieve proportionality, parents like Taliaferro could insist—and the federal government would agree—that JMU was out of compliance with the law. And as long as they were out of compliance with the law, they must add women's teams, whether or not they could afford to.

"The law forced us to take a look at our program," says James Madison's athletic director, Jeff Bourne. "When you have a program as large as ours and you're looking at proportionality, it's hard for us to come into compliance without making some cuts."

To resolve the complaint and shield itself from future lawsuits, James Madison saw no option other than to make wholesale cuts in its athletics program. Five men's teams and three women's teams were slated for elimination at the end of the 2000–01 academic year. Over a hundred athletes, many with years of eligibility left, would suddenly be downgraded from student-athlete to plain old student. The result was that fewer opportunities to play would be offered to everyone, but they would be offered in the right proportion: 58 percent for women and 42 percent for men—a mirror image of the student body. Opportunities for women wouldn't increase and opportunities for men would definitely decline, by 107 team positions. But with the plan, James Madison officials finally felt safe from future OCR complaints or lawsuits.

In the end, under pressure from alumni and students, JMU decided to reach proportionality not by out-and-out killing the teams, just by taking away all their scholarship aid. Officials eliminated scholarships in eight men's teams and four women's teams, leaving four men's and nine women's teams that receive athletic aid. The legal issue was solved, but bad feelings lingered. "Our program was healthy. We were graduating players. Our finances weren't a problem," says wrestling coach Jeff "Peanut" Bowyer, whose squad's scholarship aid was sacrificed in the cuts. "Our problem is we have 35 males on the roster at a school with a 58 percent female enrollment."

Stephen Reynolds, a senior on the men's gymnastics team, was one of those who lost his aid. It was his second Title IX athletics loss in four years. Reynolds had first attended Syracuse University, where his team was cut for the same reasons. He came to JMU hoping to finish his education with his new teammates. "This was my team, these were the people I saw every single day, for three or four hours a day. I didn't want to see my teammates go through what we did at Syracuse," says Reynolds. "Title IX was never meant to do this."

NATIONWIDE, 41 PERCENT OF college athletes are women and 56 percent of undergraduates are women. For the eager gender feminist, these statistics mean that for the entire United States to become "proportional" under Title IX—that is, for the share of female athletes to mirror the 56 percent female share of all students—the number of female athletes would need to increase by about 15 percent of all athletes, or just over 59,000. The alternative, in the binary world of Title IX, is that the number of male athletes must *decrease* by over 59,000.

What would that mean in real terms?

- eliminating every football program in the country, or,
- eliminating almost ten times the number of young men who wrestle, or,
- cutting more than the total number of men who play basketball, wrestle, run track, play tennis, swim, do gymnastics and play water polo combined.

Cuts to men's teams under Title IX proportionality are slowly moving high school and college athletics toward this feminist utopia. A look at high school athletics shows that, in contrast to the almost ninefold increase in girls, the number of boys who play sports today is just about the same as it was in 1971, having grown by less than 200,000, from 3,666,917 to 3,832,352. After decreasing significantly upon passage of Title IX, the number of boys who play sports leveled off in the 1980s and began to climb back up in the mid-1990s.

On the intercollegiate level, where Title IX enforcement has been focused, particularly in the 1990s, the record is much darker. Although about only one in sixteen high school athletes will go on to play varsity sports in college, it would be expected that male intercollegiate athletic participation would generally rise when high school participation rises, all other things being equal. Since Title IX was enacted, however, at a time when high school participation has been rising, men's involvement in intercollegiate athletics has actually dropped from 248,000 or 10.4 percent of total male undergraduates, to 234,000 or 9.5 percent of all college men.

Using data from a 1997 NCAA Gender Equity report, Leo Kocher found that more than 200 men's teams and over 20,000 male athletes disappeared from the ranks of the NCAA between 1992 and 1997. During the same period, only 5,800 women's athletic spots were added. To use the numbers-obsessed language of the Title IX feminists, this translates into 3.4 men's opportunities lost for every one opportunity gained for women.

More recent data released by the NCAA indicate that men's opportunities have actually risen in recent years. But the problem with this data is that when new schools become members of the NCAA by leaving other national collegiate associations like the National Association of Intercollegiate Athletics (NAIA) or the National Small College Athletic Association (NSCAA), they bring already existing teams with them, thus artificially inflating the "growth" of men's opportunities.

Last year, for instance, the NCAA claimed that the number of men's basketball teams in the NCAA had increased by forty-four over the previous two years. "I asked for a list of the new basketball teams and every one of those teams had been in existence for a decade or more," says Kocher. "So these were not newly created NCAA athletic opportunities for men. They were already existing and just being counted as new. That's very, very discouraging when the NCAA resorts to bogus statistics because they're the ones who keep the records."

To penetrate the tricky arithmetic of the NCAA, House Speaker Dennis Hastert, a former wrestling coach, asked the nonpartisan government General Accounting Office to look at changes in athletic opportunities for men and women. The GAO investigated the sports programs of 725 colleges and universities and found that from

1985–86 to 1996–97, 21,000 men's spots disappeared, a drop of 12 percent. Men's athletic scholarship aid declined by 10 percent. For their part, women gained 14,500 spots, a jump of 16 percent driven by a 66 percent increase in scholarships at NCAA Division I schools and a 73 percent increase at Division II colleges and universities.

The Independent Women's Forum, which has been documenting Title IX quotas in sports since 1997, keeps a running list of discontinued men's sports programs. In 1999, the total since 1992 stood at 359, including 43 wrestling teams, 53 golf programs, 16 baseball teams, 23 swimming programs and 39 tennis squads.

With the exception of football and basketball, both high-profile, revenue-generating sports, no men's program is exempted, no matter how successful or established. In 1993, UCLA, citing Title IX pressure, dropped its men's swimming and diving teams, which had produced 22 Olympic medallists, including 16 golds. Boston University ended a hundred-year-old tradition of football in 1997. Brigham Young University eliminated its top-10-ranked men's gymnastics team and its top-25-ranked wrestling team.

In the spring of 2000, the University of Miami decided to sacrifice its men's swimming program—which had sent competitors to every Olympic Games since 1972 (including gold medal winner Greg Louganis)—in order to attain Title IX proportionality. Like most colleges and universities, Miami had a growing female majority on campus that had produced a 10 percent difference between the share of students who were female and the share of athletes who were female. Administrators had elected to add, and students had agreed to fund, three new women's sports in the previous five years. But even that wasn't enough to make the numbers come out right.

"This is the most difficult decision that the athletic department has made in a very long time," said Miami athletic director Paul Dee. "These fine young men are being displaced for reasons over which they have no control and which they did not cause. It is extremely regrettable that this is the necessary solution to the issues we face."

GROUPS LIKE THE WOMEN'S SPORTS FOUNDATION and education bureaucrats maintain consistently and piously that cuts to men's programs are not the result of Title IX. The real culprits, they say, are stingy university administrators and gender-biased athletic directors. If universities would just dust off their checkbooks and fund more programs for women, they insist, they wouldn't have a problem under the law. Instead, feminists say, chauvinist administrators sacrifice nonrevenue men's teams because they refuse to spend more on women's sports, or because they refuse to cut from bloated football and men's basketball budgets.

We will turn later to the topic of football, the Title IX feminists' favorite whipping boy and ultimate target. For now, it is worth taking a hard look at the claim that men's programs are cut strictly for financial reasons.

It is true that colleges and universities are endlessly complicated financial, managerial, legal and academic enterprises. The pressure to raise money is relentless, and even in the best fundraising environment with the most generous alumni, resources are finite. Money devoted to building a new physics lab or hiring a new eighteenth-century French literature professor is money some other program or department doesn't get.

In the competition for scarce resources, Title IX has added a double burden to athletic departments. A popular misconception of the law is that it requires schools to spend equal amounts on men's and women's sports. In fact, Title IX regulations impose no such requirement. Gender equity advocates originally pushed for equal average per capita spending on male and female athletes as one of the standards of compliance, but colleges and universities were successful in having that requirement deleted from the final regulation.

They believed they had won a victory for fairness and institutional autonomy, but what they ended up with has turned out to be worse. By substituting the principle of equal participation for equal spending, Title IX has effectively made quotas the engine that pulls the "gender equity" train; proportionality in the body count drives de facto proportionality in all aspects of athletics programs. If participation must be proportionate, then the distribution of athletic scholarships must also be proportionate, and so must the provision of equipment, facilities, training, coaching and the myriad other aspects of an athletic program.

The pressure to meet participation quotas means that even when men's teams offer to become self-supporting in order to avoid being cut, universities are forced to turn a deaf ear. When Princeton and the University of Southern California found themselves on the wrong side of the proportionality requirement and moved to cut wrestling and swimming in the mid-1990s, supporters and alumni rallied to raise money to save the programs. Even so, the universities chose to cut them. Why? As Carol Zaleski, president of United States Swimming, the governing body for U.S. Olympic swimming, told a congressional committee, "It's not a question of money. It's a question of numbers."[2]

Often, the number of bodies that universities cut by eliminating men's teams so far outpaces the money they save that it is clear to coaches that they've been the victim of a numbers game, not a budget crunch. After increasing the number of female athletes on campus by 61 percent in just three years, Miami University of Ohio found itself in 1999 with a $1 million deficit in its sports program and a lingering 13-point Title IX gap. That spring, the university's trustees voted to cut men's soccer, tennis and wrestling—eliminating 30 wrestlers, 25 men's soccer players and 10 men's tennis players, who shared a total of 8 scholarships among them. The move saved $441,000, less than half of Miami's budget deficit. And it left behind a mountain of bad feeling.

The same year the cuts went into effect, the Miami women's precision skating team traveled to Europe to compete. Twice. "We went to Iowa this year and Florida," Miami wrestling coach Chuck Angello bitterly told the *Cincinnati Enquirer*. "We drove."[3]

Title IX doesn't concern itself with where funding comes from, just how it is spent. So a men's team that is particularly successful at fundraising and attracting alumni support can't spend all of the money it has raised on itself if doing so creates an imbalance between the men's and women's programs.

The Office for Civil Rights, which prides itself on being a "resource" for schools struggling to comply with Title IX, is very clear on this point. At a "gender equity" conference sponsored by the NCAA in Indianapolis in May 2000, an associate athletic director of a major Midwestern university put this question to an OCR official: A group of baseball alumni at her university was ready to write a $1.5 million check to the baseball team, she said. But the university was afraid to take the money because their softball field was located off campus. What if they take the money, she asked meekly, to build a new baseball stadium and renovate the old stadium for the softball team? Would that be permissible under the law? The OCR official shook her head. Probably not, she said. The men's and women's facilities must be exactly equivalent. And until the university could guarantee that, they couldn't accept the donation.

But the most poignant and persuasive evidence that the force driving Title IX cuts is not finances but males on the playing field is the fact that the first players to be cut are most often the walk-ons.

"Walk-on" is the term used for unrecruited players who nonetheless try out for and make varsity teams. Overwhelmingly they are men. Most often they are benchwarmers, or what the Women's Sports Foundation's Donna Lopiano likes to call "hapless practice dummies." They receive no scholarship aid. They bring their own practice gear and play for love of the game. The movie *Rudy* is based on a real-life walk-on in the Notre Dame football squad.

Virtually every men's intercollegiate athletic program in the country disallows walk-ons today under Title IX through what is euphemistically called "roster management." Both the Office for Civil Rights and the NCAA actively encourage roster management. It involves setting upper limits on the participants in men's squads and lower limits on women's squads. That invariably means turning away men who want to play and providing inducements for women, such as additional scholarships and the opportunity to become involved in "emerging sports" like equestrian and synchronized swimming.

In the fall of 1996, the University of Northern Colorado cut ten members of its wrestling team to achieve Title IX proportionality—all walk-ons. UNC football coach Joe Glenn was also forced to cut eleven nonscholarship players. The move had nothing to do with saving money, and everything to do with making the numbers line up right. "These were kids paying their own way," Glenn says. "It was the hardest, most irrational thing I've ever had to do in coaching."

ONE OF THE IRONIES OF THE proliferation of sex quotas in college and university athletic departments is that the NCAA, which began by fighting to exempt athletics from Title IX and later, failing that, to exempt revenue-producing sports like football and men's basketball, has now become a collaborator with the Department of Education in the gender-driven assault on men's athletic programs.

Each year the NCAA hosts seminars for athletic directors and members of university affirmative action bureaucracies on how to achieve "gender equity" in general and Title IX compliance in particular. One such gender equity seminar in Indianapolis in May 2000 attracted over three hundred representatives of colleges and universities, women's sports activists, legal experts and federal officials for two and a half days of discussion of Title IX. Participants listened to presentations on the law's impact on minority women, pleaded with officials for instruction on how to avoid a federal investigation, and garnered "helpful hints" on how to fill out federal forms required to measure gender equity in their sports programs. At no time was a dissenting voice raised about the bureaucratic hassles—or the systematic injustices—that the law created.

Instead, the seminar was a reflection of how deeply embedded the culture of identity politics has become in colleges and universities. Although the subject is outside the scope of Title IX, many of the presentations dealt with the representation of minorities as coaches and college administrators and in leadership positions within the NCAA itself. Also outside the scope of the law, but nonetheless discussed in detail, was the supposed need for more minority women in "nontraditional" sports such as field hockey, lacrosse, water polo, squash and tennis. These are among the sports most frequently added by institutions attempting to comply with Title IX. They are also the sports in which minority women tend not to participate.

One might assume that an NCAA seminar on Title IX compliance would focus on how to rid athletic programs of discrimination against women. But in fact the greater part of the conference was devoted to advising athletic officials on how to meet the gender quota—or, more accurately, on how to create the appearance of meeting it.

A breakout session entitled "Scholarships, Financial Aid and Roster Management" turned out to be a how-to session on manipulating the numbers of male and female athletes in order to comply with Title IX. Gender equity consultant Elaine Dreidame let the cat out of the bag when she informed her audience that although "opportunity" is a word often used in connection with Title IX, "the spirit of the law is concerned with the actual number of student-athletes who are practicing and competing." The name of the game, she counseled, is retaining female student-athletes and deterring males in order to achieve proportionality.

The statistic that federal regulators take seriously when making a threshold determination of proportionality, Driedame explained, is the number of athletes listed on the squad roster on the first day of official competition. She encouraged coaches and administrators to manipulate their schedules so as to maximize their female body count and minimize their male numbers. Most female athletes, she explained, "don't want to sit on the bench," and their numbers tend to dwindle over the course of the season as nonplaying women drop out. So Dreidame advised administrators to begin women's teams' official play in the fall, when their numbers are highest. That way, if a women's soccer squad began its season with 35 players but lost 7 over the course of the season and made the finals with only 28 players, it would still be counted as having 35 female athletes for Title IX compliance.

For the men, who have higher retention rates than women, Driedame's advice was just the opposite: consider waiting until spring to start formal competition. The boys can be counted on to stick out the practice season even if they're not sure of getting a chance to play. That way, for example, a baseball team could spend months practicing with a squad of 40, cut 10 before official competition begins and have only 30 male athletes counted toward the Title IX quota.

In her advice on how to make the sex-quota trains run on time, Dreidame matter-of-factly counseled her audience to practice roster management, but do it slowly, phasing in cuts in men's squad sizes to minimize their impact. If six slots on the wrestling squad must go, she said, cut two a year for three years, ideally by not replacing graduating seniors. She also warned that practicing roster management on women's squads by "stacking" teams with women who play multiple sports can lead to hazards in complying with athletic scholarship proportionality. Multi-sport women, she said, may add to the illusion of proportionate participation, but since each woman can receive only one scholarship, this can also lead to the appearance that the school is shortchanging women in athletic aid.

The NCAA also made sure that officials from the Office for Civil Rights were available to answer questions. Athletic directors, assistant athletic administrators, coaches, vice-presidents and Title IX compliance officers humbly asked questions and occasionally recounted horror stories brought about by their attempts to comply with the law. One administrator said that her university had recently finished constructing a new high-seating-capacity arena for its men's and women's basketball teams, but it turned out the women's team preferred to continue playing in the old, smaller gym. Because they didn't attract crowds as large as the men's team, they liked the smaller gym for the intimacy and home-court advantage it provided. Was it permissible, she asked, for the boys to move and the girls to stay? Mary Francis O'Shea, the OCR's national coordinator for athletics, responded that this was unadvisable from the federal government's standpoint; the women should be encouraged to play in the big new stadium because they probably didn't really know what they wanted. "They may think they are destined to accept the smaller crowds," O'Shea said. "They may need to be educated."

The athletic directors and other officials who attended the conference readily accepted their need to be educated as well. One participant, Brian Verigin, associate athletic director at Northern Michigan University, seemed to be genuinely committed to providing opportunities in sports for women on his campus. Northern Michigan, he explained, had ranked in the bottom ten schools in Title IX compliance (measured in terms of their proximity to proportionality) by the *Chronicle of Higher Education* in 1998. After cutting wrestling, men's gymnastics and men's cross-country and offering the maximum number of women's sports, the school finally achieved the coveted statistical balance in its program.

Verigin, who like everyone else in the room had not questioned any of the requirements of proportionality during the presentation, believed his university was doing the right thing. But he acknowledged that their efforts to comply with Title IX had created new inequities in his sports program. "I have a football team that only travels by bus, sometimes 16 or 17 hours to a game," he said. "Meanwhile our [women's] volleyball team takes charter flights to at least two games a year. Is that fair? How can I look my football coach in the eye and say that's fair?"

I asked Verigin if he believed there had been discrimination against women at Northern Michigan when women were still the "underrepresented sex" on campus. "The problem was that back then we didn't even know we had a problem," he said. "It's only more recently that we've come to realize that we had a problem. We needed to be educated."

Northern Michigan's education came in the form of an OCR compliance review in 1993, a top-to-bottom federal audit of their athletics program initiated by the OCR in the absence of any complaint about discrimination. Since then, the school has dropped three men's teams and earned a clean bill of health. Like his fellow conference-goers, Verigin was loath to question the value of "gender equity," even as he acknowledged its costs. "We've made a lot of progress," he said, "but there is reverse discrimination going on."

DEFENDERS OF TITLE IX QUOTAS like to argue that none of this bloodshed would be necessary if it weren't for one thing: football. This sport is the feminists' ultimate target because of its symbolic association with raw maleness. They know they can't get rid of football, but they can at least hold it responsible for Title IX's impact on other men's sports. Not only does football cost too much, they say, but it is the biggest, most powerful redoubt of white male hostility to leveling the playing field for women. When men's teams get cut, they say, the real culprit is football. "If you cut a men's team and blame it on women that's an easier argument than saying we've been indulgent, we're spending too much on football," says Women's Sports Foundation founder Donna deVarona.

Supporters of football argue that the revenue and excitement generated by the sport are the lifeline that keeps many women's teams and men's nonrevenue sports alive. On the other side are people like deVarona, joined by some men's minor sports supporters, who say that football is the black hole of intercollegiate athletics: resources fall into it, never to be seen again. "Football is not the golden goose," says Donna Lopiano, executive director of the Women's Sports Foundation. "It's a fat goose eating food that could nourish more opportunities for women."[4]

Perhaps fittingly, given this animus, the first time that Title IX was mentioned in the same breath as athletics, the subject was football. The late Senator John Tower of Texas tried twice to pass an amendment to the law to exempt "revenue-producing sports" (read: football) from its provisions. Tower, who was a co-sponsor of the original Title IX legislation, worried that the government, "in its laudable zeal to guarantee equal athletic opportunities to women, is defeating its own purpose by promulgating rules which will damage the financial base of intercollegiate athletics."[5]

The Tower amendment was never passed, and football remains the fat man tipping the canoe of Title IX, a unique obstacle to achieving numerical gender balance in intercollegiate athletic programs. Activists such as Lopiano complain about the resources football consumes, but the real problem is the bodies it supports. At the most competitive level of play, the NCAA Division I-A level, squads typically carry more than 100 players and are allowed 85 scholarships. That's over 100 slots on the male side of the proportionality ledger for which there is no female equivalent. In the binary mathematics of Title IX, this means that schools must have four or five additional women's teams just to "make up" for the numbers added to the men's count by football.

Fresno State University, because it has a football team, was unable to comply with a court order mandating that it reach proportionality by 1998—even though it eliminated two other men's teams, added two women's teams and offered the maximum number of scholarships to its female athletes allowed by NCAA rules. In every sport except basketball, in which men and women received the same number of scholarships, Fresno offered women more scholarship aid. Still, because of the 85 scholarships offered for football, the school couldn't reach the court-ordered quota. In 1998, Fresno appealed to the NCAA to relax its limitation on athletic scholarships in order to attract more women to its programs. The NCAA refused.

Title IX quota enthusiasts have used the fashionable criticism of an "arms race" in collegiate athletic expenditures, led by big-time football, to help make their case for mandated higher expenditures for women. This argument states that the push for competitive advantage in collegiate football (and the television contracts and alumni dollars that flow to winning teams) is fueling a spiral of profligacy on college campuses that is bankrupting athletic departments. In their desperation to produce winning teams, colleges and universities are pouring money into football programs that should go to women's teams. All this spending, so the argument goes, isn't paying off in winning teams and sufficient revenue to cover the high costs of football for most schools. Still, they keep pouring money into the pigskin money pit in a desperate attempt to outbid their rivals.

While it is true that expenditures in intercollegiate athletics are rising, for both men's and women's programs, the gender-equity landscape in collegiate athletic expenditures and revenues is much more complicated than the "blame football first" argument suggests. In fact, the most recent survey of the finances of NCAA member institutions shows a widening gap between profit-making athletic departments and revenue-losing athletic departments—with no correlation to the presence or absence of football.

The study, undertaken by the *Chronicle of Higher Education,* found that 64 percent of schools in Division I-A, reported making a profit in their football programs. In their overall athletic budgets, Division I-A schools with football tended to break even whereas schools without football lost an average of $2.5 million. Smaller Division I schools with football teams, in Division I-AA, reported losses averaging $2.2 million. At a lower competitive level within the NCAA, Division II, colleges and universities with and without football lost money on athletics.[6]

An exhaustive study of the business of intercollegiate sports by the *Philadelphia Inquirer* confirms that programs are sharply divided between the haves and the have-nots. The *Inquirer* found that the 114 schools of Division I-A accounted for 6 of every 10 dollars in intercollegiate athletic revenue. That leaves about 800 colleges and universities to split the remaining 40 percent of revenue. The paper looked at the top 50 intercollegiate football programs and found that they made total profits of $403 million in 1999—an average of $8 million each. That translates into an average profit margin of 50 percent.[7]

Football programs spend money in addition to earning money, of course. Using data from the 1996–97 academic year, University of Arizona economics professor R. Bruce Billings calculated that Division I-A football programs on average earn 43 percent of all sports revenues and incur 26 percent of total sports costs. The same analysis shows that the number two revenue-producing sport, men's basketball, earns 16.1 percent of average total revenues while incurring 7.5 percent of average total costs.[8] These revenues over expenses go back into the system to fund other programs.

Feminists decry the high costs of big-time football programs as if they were robbing the budgets of women's sports. In fact, according to an analysis done by the *Chronicle of Higher Education,* it is the "have" schools, whose budgets are bursting with "tainted" profits from football and men's basketball, that do the best job of providing opportunities and spending for women's athletes.

The schools that belong to what the *Chronicle* calls the "equity" conferences with big-time football and basketball television contracts and bowl games—the Atlantic Coast, Big East, Big Ten, Big 12, Pacific-10 and Southeastern conferences—are those that field the largest and most diverse women's sports programs. These schools earn big profits from football and smaller profits from men's basketball, profits that eventually find their way to women's teams. In these conferences, women are over 50 percent of students and 42 percent of athletes.[9] In contrast, in the smaller, regional colleges and universities of Division II, women are over 55 percent of students and only 38 percent of athletes. In the still smaller, nonscholarship athletic programs of NCAA Division III, women are 41 percent of athletes while also constituting a majority of the students.[10]

Professor Billings looked at the data and found a direct correlation between football profits and "gender equity." Although the size of a school's endowment and whether it is a state or a private institution also has some correlation with proportionality in its athletic program, Billings found that football profits make a big difference, especially in financial aid. Compliance increases by .4 percentage points for each $1 million in football profits. With some institutions earning as much as $10 million a year, this can be a significant influence in the aid that supports "gender equity."

The upshot is that feminists tread on dangerous ground when they seek to demonize football with their frequent charges that a) it doesn't make as much money as Title IX quota critics claim it does, and b) it's too expensive. The same *Philadelphia Inquirer* study that showed the unequal distribution of wealth in collegiate athletic programs also found that women's sports kick very little into the coffers. Basketball is the female glamour sport, the women's equivalent of football. Yet according to the study, the top 100 women's basketball teams in the country lost a total of $65 million in 1999 (while men's basketball at the same schools made $150 million). The exception is the national champion University of Connecticut team, which has that rare thing in women's sports, a television contract. In 1999 the lady Huskies made $1 million.[11] And in terms of costs, a 1997 *USA Today* study of gender equity found that NCAA schools spent more to field the average women's basketball player than the average football player. The analysis reported that schools spent $39,892 for each female basketball player and $28,999 per football player. Female athletes in sports other than basketball were also more expensive for schools than males in sports other than football: $10,867 per athlete compared with $7,767.[12]

Feminists can't clamor for protections and preferences for women's programs in federal law while at the same time demanding that men's programs alone be justified on a profit-making basis. But clamor they do, and at the root of their grievance is a deep antipathy for football and the macho traditions it carries with it. This is why they are willing to claim that the elimination of men's teams under Title IX is a conspiracy orchestrated by big-time football.

"It's a very clever strategy to have men's minor sports being pitted against women," said Mary Jo Kane, director of the Tucker Center for Research on Girls and Women in Sport at the University of Minnesota. "The irony in all this is that if men's nonrevenue sports would team up with women's sports and go after football, [reducing] the size and expenditures in football, you could add sports for women and very comfortably support men's nonrevenue sports."

But taking on the sport that fills the stadiums, brings in the television contracts and fuels the romantic myth of intercollegiate athletics is, to put it simply, not a winning strategy for men's sports hurt by Title IX. University of Chicago wrestling coach Leo Kocher believes that putting the breaks on the escalating arms race over college football is a worthy goal—and completely beside the point in the "gender equity" debate.

> If people want to pass legislation that tells Notre Dame that they must spend less on a football program that brings in tens of millions of dollars—good luck. But big-time college football doing with less will not make more women want to play collegiate sports. It will not change the fact that Division III men's baseball teams cut dozens of players in order to get their average squad size down to 30.4 players while women's NCAA softball teams struggle to get their average squad up to 18.

Many women, too, see that buying into the bellicose rhetoric of gender activists is self-defeating. Female athletes on campus—if not feminist ideologues in the faculty lounge—understand that their fate, more often than not, is intertwined with that of their male counterparts. Time and again the first group to raise their voices to protest men's Title IX cuts are the women who have traveled with and practiced alongside the men all year. In addition to the camaraderie they feel, these female athletes understand that success in their men's athletic department is good for women. It opens doors to hugely successful programs like the women's soccer team at the University of North Carolina at Chapel Hill, for example, which is underwritten with money made by men's basketball, and the University of Tennessee women's basketball team, a dynasty whose seed money came from Tennessee football. Some of these women's programs have gone on to be more successful than the men's programs that provided their genesis. Perhaps one day the University of Connecticut women's basketball team will help underwrite a national champion men's baseball team. When that day comes, it will be a victory for hard work and common sense, not for the us-versus-them philosophy of "gender equity."

THE FLIP SIDE OF ELIMINATING opportunities for men to meet Title IX quotas, of course, is the push to entice new women onto the playing field. In many cases, this has resulted in legitimate new opportunities for young women to enjoy the physical and educational benefits of athletics. In too many other cases, however, the rush to make athletes out of uninspired and inexperienced young women in the name of "gender equity" has resulted in new inequities and the athletic equivalent of a charade.

In 1993, the same year its Gender Equity Task Force declared proportionality the "ultimate goal" of NCAA member institutions, the NCAA identified nine "emerging sports" for women to help schools meet the numerical requirement of proportionality. Colleges and universities, said the Gender Equity Task Force, should add at least two additional women's sports from a list of exotic athletic endeavors like synchronized swimming, team handball, water polo, archery, badminton, bowling, ice hockey and squash. Equestrian, initially overlooked, was added in 1998.

The term "emerging sports" implies that these activities were increasingly pursued by girls in high schools. By adding them to their programs, so the theory went, colleges and universities would not just be engaged in gender bean-counting but would actually be fulfilling the legitimate athletic aspirations of thousands of young girls.

The problem was that very few girls were engaged in any of the NCAA's list of "emerging sports" in 1994. Only 11 high schools in the nation offered archery teams. Just 28 schools had equestrian squads. Fewer than 200 individual girls played ice hockey. And a survey by the National Federation of State High School Associations failed to report the existence of a single high school girls' synchronized swimming, handball or squash team.

Still, with the NCAA's encouragement, colleges and universities began to pour resources into these sports with the hope of attracting sufficient numbers of women to athletics to make their quotas. Adding the twelve women necessary to create a synchronized swimming or a handball team, however, didn't result in sufficient additions to their female body count. The numbers just weren't adding up fast enough. Also, fielding successful teams in these sports required finding women who had experience prior to entering college, a difficult and sometimes impossible task. What they needed, athletic directors realized, was a sport that could accommodate large numbers of women and didn't require previous experience. And there it was, tucked in among the NCAA list of "emerging sports": crew.

From the beginning, women's rowing has occupied a special niche in the history of Title IX. In 1976, twenty members of the Yale women's rowing team, with a *New York Times* reporter in tow, marched into the athletics office to protest their second-class treatment at the university. They read a statement decrying Yale's lack of shower facilities for women's crew members, and then stripped to the waist, revealing the words "Title IX" written on each woman's back and breasts.

When the story ran in the March 4, 1976, edition of the *Times*, it set off what the newspaper later called an "international reaction." Within two weeks, female rowers at Yale had new locker rooms. The event—and the story of one of the rowers, Chris Ernst, who went on to become a two-time Olympic rower—was later portrayed in a film called *A Hero for Daisy*.

By 1994, the days when women's crew teams were left to shiver in the cold while the men showered in the boathouse were a distant memory. Attracted by squad sizes that start at 60 but can reach as high as 200, schools began pouring resources into creating women's rowing programs. The NCAA sanctioned 20 scholarships per team, the highest of any women's sport. And from just 66 programs in 1995, the number of intercollegiate women's rowing teams almost doubled in four years, to 122 in 1999. "The reason we're here—everybody knows it—is for gender equity," said University of Massachusetts women's rowing coach Jim Deitz in 1999.[13]

Complicating the challenge for women's crew coaches like Deitz was the fact that the pool of experienced high school female rowers he has to recruit from is small and showing little signs of growth. In 1994, the year rowing was designated an "emerging sport" by the NCAA, there were only 36 high school girls' teams nationwide. In the years since then, according to the National Federation of State High School Associations, while the number of intercollegiate women's squads has almost doubled, the number of high school teams has actually shrunk, to 34.

This means that coaches like Deitz have routinely had to offer spots on rowing squads, and most often full scholarships to go with them, to women who have never before touched an oar. Schools have been forced to hold open try-outs in which any woman can come and join the team. And although some coaches question how often the last 80 or so women on a 150-woman squad get to compete—or even if they show up regularly at the boathouse to practice—coaches have instituted "no-cut" policies, all in an effort to attract and keep females on their rosters.

In a devastating profile of the lengths to which some schools are going to cobble together women's rowing teams, the *Wall Street Journal* reported that some coaches are literally walking through the campus in search of tall, broad-shouldered women, recruiting novices in stairwells, campus lunchrooms and even off-campus diners. When the University of Kansas added women's crew to achieve proportionality under Title IX in the late 1990s, they had no high school rowing teams in the Midwest from which to recruit. The athletic director was forced to make an appeal at freshman orientation and managed to convince over a hundred women to try out for the team. At Ohio State they went even further and put an ad in the student newspaper: "Tall athletic women wanted. No experience necessary!"

As schools without a tradition of crew or even access to a body of water seek to create teams (Arizona State University, in the desert city of Tempe, famously flooded a two-mile stretch of dry gulch to provide a place for its new team to practice), coaches are having to look to Canada, Europe and Australia to find experienced rowers. Some coaches are resorting to recruiting basketball and volleyball players who aren't good enough to earn scholarships in their own sports. But even this outreach often falls short. "We're not getting some of those athletes because, with so many scholarships out there, other schools are offering them full rides," confessed University of Washington women's crew coach Jan Harville in 2000.[14]

Even when the teams and the scholarship aid are available, qualified females—both athletically and academically—can be hard to find. San Diego State University learned this the hard way when it failed to comply with the terms of a consent decree ordering all of the schools in the California State University to achieve proportionality by the 1998–99 school year. San Diego budgeted the scholarship aid and the necessary funds for its athletic program to match its 55-percent-female student body but couldn't find enough academically qualified athletes to take the money. The school even created a summer school for female athletes who were in need of academic remediation, yet in the words of the CSU/Cal-NOW Consent Decree Final Report, "not enough qualified student-athletes accepted the offer."[15]

The premise of Title IX proportionality is that girls and women, given the opportunity, will participate in athletics at the same rate as men. But for the time being at least, it appears that women need to be offered more scholarship aid than men just to participate at their current rate of about 40 percent of collegiate athletes. Why, if all this scholarship money is going into women's sports, do women stubbornly refuse to participate at the same rate as men?

In 1993 a court ordered the California State University at Northridge to achieve Title IX proportionality in its athletic program

within five years, forcing CSUN administrators to cut their men's soccer, baseball, swimming and volleyball teams.* Proportionality
proponents said the failure of the school's athletic program to mirror
its student body was the result of illegal discrimination against
women.

But CSUN president Blenda Wilson saw other, less insidious forces
at work. "I was at our football game last weekend and I said to a col-
league of mine as we looked at what must have been a hundred men
lined up in red, black and white jerseys along the sidelines for Cal
State Northridge," Wilson told PBS's *National Desk.* "I said, that's a
part of the gender-equity problem. There is no sport where a hundred women will stand along the sidelines when only twenty-two get
to play."

It's an often-heard complaint from coaches of women's sports that
although there are many fiercely dedicated female athletes, fewer
women than men are willing to "ride the bench" for a season without getting a chance to compete. "There's an expectation that there
are all these women out there to choose from now. They're all coming out of high school where they participated in sports," CSUN head
softball coach Janet Sherman told PBS. "But they don't want to sit the
bench. I can't get the women to come out. I can't change that."

"Girls are smarter," says Providence College women's tennis coach
Carl LaBranche, who lost his men's team to Title IX cuts in 1998.
"They look at the other girls playing and in some cases they say, I'm
not going to be number nine or number ten. So even though we
have twelve spots [on the team] I can't fill them because the girls ask,
'How many travel?' We say, 'Eight.' And they say, 'That's okay coach.
Nice knowing you.'"[16]

Because women are less willing to ride the bench—and less willing
to "walk on" to a team and play without receiving an athletic scholarship—women's team sizes tend to be smaller than men's,
complicating the task of reaching numerical parity in an athletic program. Even today, when the overwhelming majority of men's teams

*The outcry prompted by the elimination of four men's teams was such that the
California state legislature intervened and passed legislation providing funding
for the men's teams for an additional year, and the men's teams were eventually
reinstated. Meanwhile, women became 60 percent of Northridge students but the
percentage of women expressing interest in sports remained stuck at 38 percent.
As of February 2000, Northridge had not met the terms of the Cal-NOW consent
decree.

have been artificially limited in the number of players they can carry, the average squad size of men's intercollegiate teams is larger than that of women's teams. While a women's indoor track team on average consists of 27 players, a men's team will attract over 32; typically 22 women will come out for lacrosse, but 31 men will make the same commitment; and women's softball coaches get around 18 participants, whereas over 30 men are drawn to the baseball team.

The result is that schools must offer more sports to women than to men, just to get equal numbers of athletes of both sexes coming out to play. Nationally, NCCA member schools offer women 553 more athletic programs to choose from than they offer to men. And still, fewer women participate in intercollegiate sports than men— about 77,000 fewer in 1998–99.

Title IX quota advocates answer the claim that women are less interested than men in athletic competition by saying that such assertions have always been the stock in trade of the patriarchy—and they have a point. It wasn't so long ago that women were denied the opportunity to play sports on the basis of the rock-solid conventional wisdom that they weren't interested in athletics, which were "unfeminine."

Today, a new but not altogether different conventional wisdom holds sway among proponents of Title IX proportionality. It, too, judges women as a group, not as individuals, and it, too, seeks to tell women what their interests and capabilities are instead of allowing them to define those for themselves. Its adherents aren't the male-dominated athletics establishment of old, but the effect is still the same. Much as the patriarchy robbed women of their self-determination in the bad old days, today the government, the courts and the women's groups, acting through the agency of American educational institutions, are seeking to make girls' and women's decisions for them.

THREE

IF YOU BUILD IT, THEY WILL COME: THE BROWN DECISION

The one constant through all the years, Ray, has been baseball. America has rolled by like an army of steam-rollers. It's been erased like a blackboard, rebuilt, and erased again. But baseball has marked the time. This field, this game, is part of our past, Ray. It reminds us of all that once was good, and that could be good again. Oh people will come, Ray. People will most definitely come.
— The Field of Dreams

THE LAST THING ON BROWN University president Vartan Gregorian's mind in the spring of 1991 was a lawsuit alleging sex discrimination in sports on his campus. Since going coed with the absorption of Pembroke College in 1971, Brown, the archetypically liberal Ivy League institution, had created an exemplary array of sports opportunities for its female students. Brown women had 15 sports teams to choose from, almost twice the average of 8.3 for other NCAA Division I schools. Only one school, Harvard, had a broader and more generous women's athletic program.

But like most university presidents in the early 1990s, Gregorian was struggling with budget pressures. Faced with a $1.6 million operating shortfall, he ordered cuts across the board. For athletic director David Roach, Gregorian's mandate meant cutting $79,000 of his $5 million budget. So Roach chose what he believed was the fairest and most equitable method: two men's teams and two women's teams—men's golf and water polo and women's volleyball and gymnastics—were downgraded from university-funded varsity status to partially funded status. The athletes could still play and remained eligible to compete in NCAA tournaments, but they would have to pitch in to raise some of their own funds to do so.

Brown's cost-cutting measure might have been lost in the generalized austerity that hit higher education in the early 1990s if it weren't for what happened next. On February 26, 1992, the Supreme Court ruled that Christine Franklin was eligible for money damages from the Gwinnett County School District in Georgia for a Title IX sexual harassment claim she had filed a year earlier. Franklin charged that the district had failed to protect her from sexual advances by her high school economics teacher. She said the teacher had repeatedly asked that she be excused from class, whereupon he would take her to a private office and force her to have sex. When she reported the behavior, school officials did nothing. The upshot, she claimed, was that the school district owed her punitive damages for her teacher's harassing behavior. The high court agreed, and for the first time it became possible for women and their lawyers to go to court under Title IX and receive not only redress of their grievances, but compensatory money damages as well.

The *Franklin* decision was like a dinner bell sounding in the gender-feminist law community. Overnight, the potential for generous money damages made the pursuit of "gender equity" attractive to a new group of litigants. Lawsuits alleging sex discrimination under Title IX sprang up across the country, many of them driven by one man: Arthur Bryant, executive director of an organization called Trial Lawyers for Public Justice.

Bryant and the TLPJ had racked up a string of successful Title IX actions against colleges and universities in the early 1990s by staying out of the papers and out of court. In a typical case, Bryant would approach a university on behalf of a women's team that had been cut and demand that the team be reinstated—and that he be compensated for his time in making the request. If the school refused, Bryant promised to take it to court. But things never went that far. Eager to avoid the bad publicity and expense of a Title IX lawsuit, college administrators uniformly gave in to Bryant's demands. The University of New Hampshire, the University of Oklahoma, the College of William and Mary and the University of Massachusetts all reversed decisions to cut women's teams after being threatened with a Title IX lawsuit by TPLJ. The women got their teams; Bryant got his attorney's fees.

To Bryant, Brown seemed at first to be yet another opportunity to get yet another university administrator to roll over on Title IX quotas. "What we expected—what Arthur expected—was that this would be one of many that you've never heard about where the call was made, the letter was sent, the meeting was held, and the damage was undone," says Lynette Labinger, a Providence lawyer who tried the case with Bryant. "No one expected that Brown would want to draw a line in the sand and say: cross it."

But Bryant encountered a different breed of university administrator in Vartan Gregorian. "We got a letter in December of 1991 from Arthur Bryant stating that the women were being cut and that wasn't allowable. And if we would just reinstate them and pay him some money for attorney's fees, they [TLPJ] would go away," recalls Brown general counsel Beverly Ledbetter, who oversaw the case for the university. Gregorian, says Ledbetter, "was incensed by that. He was the kind of person that if you came to him, he would always make things better for you. But he didn't like people going behind his back. And he didn't like people attacking an institution for their own gain."

Gregorian refused to settle, so the case went to court. And for conservative critics of identity politics, it seemed at first a delicious irony that Brown University, wrapped as it was in an unspotted mantle of political correctness, would find itself suddenly dropped behind enemy lines in the gender wars. But the targeting of Brown had been no accident. The person responsible for bringing the Brown case to Bryant and the TLPJ was Kathryn Reith, a Brown alumna and director of advocacy for the Women's Sports Foundation. From the WSF's offices in Manhattan, Reith had been laboring for months and getting nowhere encouraging female athletes to file federal complaints alleging Title IX violations for a lack of proportionality in their athletic programs. Then the *Franklin* decision opened up a new, more lucrative and more hopeful route to the WSF's political goals. Together, Reith and Bryant went shopping for a client at Brown. They settled on Amy Cohen, the former captain of the ill-fated gymnastics team.

After signing up Cohen and eight members of the downgraded women's teams, Bryant and his feminist allies set out to make Brown an example of a new regime of Title IX enforcement. The university, they conceded, had an exemplary program of women's athletics. No one was saying that women weren't being given their fair share of equipment, coaching, practice time and facilities. Nor could anyone complain that Brown women were receiving fewer athletic scholarships than their male counterparts, since the university offered no athletic aid to begin with. Bryant and Labinger couldn't even argue that women had fewer sports teams than men at Brown, because women's varsity teams outnumbered men's teams.

What Amy Cohen's attorneys did argue was the fact that women at Brown participated in sports at lower rates than men, and therefore were discriminated against. At the time the lawsuit was filed, 51 percent of Brown students were women but "only" 38–39 percent of Brown athletes were women. The university's supposedly evenhanded demotion of two men's teams along with women's volleyball and gymnastics, Bryant and Labinger contended, wasn't evenhanded at all. It merely perpetuated a preexisting inequity. One of the plaintiffs, former gymnast Eileen Rocchio, succinctly illustrated the obsession with numbers behind the case in a statement to *USA Today:* "The athletes at Brown are 61 percent male. It doesn't take a rocket scientist, or a Brown degree, to see that's not equal."[1]

Brown would present reams of data attempting to show that women on campus participated in sports at a lower rate than men because they had a lower level of interest in athletics than men. But Amy Cohen and the other plaintiffs would argue that such data were irrelevant. They would make what they called a "field of dreams" argument, the phrase coming from the 1989 movie in which Kevin Costner stars as a farmer-mystic haunted by dreams of baseball, a lost father and personal wholeness. "If you build it, they will come," voices tell Costner, instructing him to build a baseball diamond in his cornfield. The university's responsibility under Title IX, the Brown plaintiffs charged, was the same as Costner's. If they created the teams, hired the coaches and built the facilities, women would play. Brown's mandate under the law, then, was not just to accommodate women who were interested in sports, but to cultivate athleticism in women who didn't yet know they were interested.

"I'm asked all the time whether the interests and abilities of women are met," said Donna Lopiano, executive director of the Women's Sports Foundation and a star witness for the plaintiffs. "There's never been a question of enough interest. If you build it, they will come."[2] The duty of the universities and colleges of America, then, was not to fulfill demand, but to *create* it.

At stake in the case was not just Brown's guilt or innocence under this standard, but the guilt or innocence of virtually every institution of higher learning in America. For if Brown—with double the average number of women's teams—was not in compliance with the law, then no school in the country was. "It was a win-win situation" for Amy Cohen and her lawyers, says Brown defense attorney Jeff Michaelson. "If they lost they could always say that this was a tough case but that other schools are going to be easier. And if they won, they won."

"In the end," says Michaelson, "it probably turned out to be a good strategy."

FROM THE OUTSET OF *Cohen v. Brown,* the portents for the defense were bad. Before the trial even began, senior First Circuit Court judge Raymond J. Pettine ordered Brown to restore funding for the two demoted women's teams pending the outcome of the case. Brown appealed, and the first appeals court ruling on Title IX in intercollegiate athletics was made—turning them down. The appeals court judge ruled that budget deficits were no excuse for cutting women's teams. Title IX required Brown to satisfy all female interest in athletics on campus "even if it requires [the university] to give the underrepresented gender (in this case women) what amounts to a larger slice of a shrinking athletic-opportunity pie."

Thus encouraged, in the trial on the merits Arthur Bryant and Lynette Labinger (who had once been Judge Pettine's clerk) made a simple argument for Brown's guilt under the federal bureaucracy's interpretation of the statute. The university, they contended, failed each and every part of the 1979 policy interpretation's three-part test. On the first test, proportionality, Brown was a clear failure. Although an impressive 38 percent of Brown athletes were female, women comprised 51 percent of the student body. In the statistics-driven logic of gender politics, this added up to a Title IX gap of 13 points. Even the Brown defense was forced to concede that Brown did not meet the proportionality standard.

Having lost the assumption of compliance with Title IX that comes with meeting the proportionality standard, Brown had to prove its innocence with one of the remaining two tests. But under prong two, which asks if a school has shown a history of continuous expansion of women's opportunities to play sports, the university didn't fare much better. Brown had created the bulk of its women's athletics program in the 1970s, immediately after going coed. Brown argued that this early expansion of female athletic opportunity—which was so thorough that it left few women's sports to be added in 1991—was a measure of its commitment to opportunity for women. Bryant and Labinger, however, regarded it as evidence of quite the opposite. The university, they argued, hadn't added a new women's team since 1982. Since it had no history of "continuous" expansion of women's opportunities, compliance under prong two of the three-part test was out of the question.

That left the third test as Brown's last hope for prevailing under the federal regulations: whether its athletics program, as it was currently constructed, satisfied those Brown women who had the interest and ability to play varsity sports. Bryant and Labinger argued that on this test, too, Brown failed. The very fact that the university had de-funded two viable women's teams, they told the court, was proof that it had failed to accommodate the interests of potential female athletes at Brown. "Our legal case was simple," says Labinger. "Here are students. They participate in gymnastics. They participate in women's volleyball. They were successful and capable of sustaining successful teams. They were available to compete and they could not [compete] as donor-funded or club sports."

The same argument could be made for the two downgraded men's teams as well, of course. But it was the central contention of the Cohen legal team in the Brown case that men's athletic interests and abilities quite literally didn't matter. Satisfying the interests of women, they argued, didn't mean providing sports opportunities for them to the same degree as they were provided for men. It meant providing opportunities for *all* interested women athletes, even at the cost of reducing opportunities for men. The fact that more men may be interested in sports to begin with didn't enter into the equation. As long as participation of female and male athletes at Brown failed to mirror exactly their proportions in the student body, women's opportunities to play sports must at all times come before men's. Or, as Bryant told the *Chronicle of Higher Education,* "If a school wants to eliminate teams before women have their fair share, it can only eliminate men's teams."[3]

Amy Cohen's argument was a transformational expansion of the meaning of the three-part test—and it was an argument that rested on the notion of women as passive victims in a world still dominated by masculine power. Where Congress had originally spoken of providing athletic opportunities to men and women equally, Amy Cohen's lawyers were arguing for an explicit preference for women. The rationale they offered for this preference was the heart of their "field of dreams" theory of the case: Trying to determine what women's interests in athletics were and whether they were greater or lesser than men's was a waste of time. It didn't matter what women perceived their interests to be when they got to Brown because, as women, their interests had never been allowed to develop fully. How could a girl know she was interested in being a synchronized swimmer if the male-dominated society had always denied her the opportunity to be one?

And because Brown, by its financial and administrative decisions, determined who played sports, there was no reason for Brown not to give every preference to women—short of dragging them onto the playing field by force—to see that they participated at the same rate as men. Moreover, the plaintiffs contended, Brown could not hide behind the defense that there were unfilled positions on women's teams—that it had created opportunities on teams that women simply chose not to take advantage of. To be meaningful, "opportunities" had to mean actual women on the playing field, not "theoretical" opportunities for which there were no female takers. Brown's obligation wasn't simply to present opportunities to women and allow them to choose, because the very notion that women have a choice is an illusion, they argued.

"Brown, like other universities, predetermines men's and women's athletic participation rates through its sports offerings, team sizes, coaches, recruiting and admission practices," Labinger wrote in the *New York Times*. "In other words, if there is a 'quota' involved here, it's established by the school, not Title IX."[4]

The plaintiffs called Donald Sabo, a self-proclaimed feminist theorist and professor of sociology at D'Youville College, to put their new version of Title IX in its proper postmodern perspective. The word "interest," Sabo told the court, is "dubious." Merely asking a woman whether or not she is interested in sports, he testified, fails to take into account the historical, social and political "contextualization" of women's role in society. These influences, he said, "either sustain or disdain, augment or dement [*sic*] people's interest in athletics." In other words, according to Sabo and the Brown plaintiffs, women didn't have interests of their own; their interests were determined for them by society. And because society has historically shortchanged women, it is left to colleges and universities under Title IX to do something about it by determining those interests in the direction of sports.

Brown's part in correcting societal discrimination against women, argued Amy Cohen's lawyers, could be accomplished by re-funding the women's gymnastics and volleyball teams and continuing to create teams until women reached statistical proportionality. Brown president Vartan Gregorian disagreed vehemently. "By judicial fiat," he thundered, women's athletics "have risen past all other priorities including undergraduate scholarship, faculty salaries and libraries." The only choice, he concluded, was to fight Amy Cohen's case as an abuse of judicial discretion and a misapplication of the law.[5]

IT WAS ONLY THE SECOND DAY of the trial in Judge Pettine's courtroom when it became clear to the Brown defense that it was arguing not to prevail in the First Circuit, but to make a case for an eventual Supreme Court review. When Walter B. Connolly Jr., a lawyer for the university, asked Judge Pettine to keep an "open mind" about Brown's interpretation of the three-part test, Pettine replied that he would be "amazed" if he were to agree with Connolly. "That would not be interpretation," the judge said. "That would be lawlessness."

Despite this prejudicial response, Brown attorneys Connolly and Jeff Michaelson forged ahead with their argument. While the Cohen plaintiffs had looked to the three-part test to make their case, the Brown defense went back to the words of Title IX itself. Brown's argument was historic because the university chose not to argue that it had met the criteria of the three-part test but to challenge the validity of the test itself. The congressional authors of the law, Connolly and Michaelson argued, forbade quotas when they added the provision taken from the 1964 Civil Rights Act. This section, they maintained, explicitly forbade what Amy Cohen said was required.

Because the three-part test was based on a misinterpretation of the law, the Brown defense argued, the court should not grant it deference in deciding Brown's guilt or innocence. And besides being a quota, the defense argued, the proportionality test offered no reliable measure of whether a school discriminates. Just because a school has an athletics program that mirrors its student body, said defense attorneys Michaelson and Connolly, does not necessarily mean it isn't discriminating against women, just as a school's failure to achieve the required sex ratio doesn't mean that it is. Michaelson remarks:

> It just doesn't follow that proportionality in any activity proves that you're not discriminating. It's not true for racial discrimination, it's not true for religious discrimination, and it's not true for athletic participation. We argued that because Title IX doesn't apply just to athletics—if you look at an engineering program or a dance program, for whatever reason you're going to find a disproportion of men in engineering and a disproportionate number of women in the dance—why would you assume that disproportion in sports indicates discrimination?

The defense introduced survey data collected from students who had applied to Brown, showing that 91 percent of applicants who said they were interested in dance were women, 56 percent of those who indicated an interest in drama were women, and 66 percent of those who expressed an interest in music were women. No one was arguing that the sex ratio in these programs should mirror the overall enrollment numbers. No one was talking about decreasing the opportunities for women in dance. Why were they singling out sports?

To pull the philosophical rug out from under proportionality as a measure of discrimination, the defense had to make the case that there were perfectly reasonable and non-bias-related reasons why women and men participated in sports at different rates at Brown. The argument they settled on was simple, but explosively controversial. "Studies have shown that women are not as interested as men in participating in sports," Connolly told the court as the Brown defense began.[6]

The Brown defense backed up this assertion by showing that on every level of athletic activity offered at Brown, men participated at a higher rate than women. On intramural teams—purely recreational teams on which anyone who wanted to could come out and play—men outnumbered women by three to one. And in Brown club sports (self-funded teams not eligible for NCAA competition), Connolly showed, men outplayed women by an even higher ratio: eight to one.

But what of those students interested and able to compete at the higher, varsity intercollegiate level? The Brown defense presented survey after survey showing that the current ratio of female to male varsity athletes at Brown—40 percent to 60 percent—matched the differing levels of interest among Brown students. And these were not casual studies. "Most election-year surveys that turn out to be accurate are done by sampling less than 1 percent of the population," says Beverly Ledbetter, who supervised the Brown defense. "We sampled 10 percent of the population at Brown. We found that interest in sports was about the same as the participation level. And to the extent that students expressed a desire to compete in sports that weren't available, that too broke down at a 60/40 male/female ratio."

Michaelson and Connolly also presented data showing that not only current Brown students, but high school students who were just thinking about coming to Brown and playing athletics also broke down at about 40 percent female and 60 percent male. They brought in Brian O'Reilly, director of SAT Operations and Development at the College Board, to testify that voluntary surveys filled out by students who applied to Brown showed that 60 percent who expressed an interest in competing in varsity athletics were male and 40 percent were female.[7]

The point, Brown's attorneys argued, was that Brown had to deal with the interests of students as it found them, not as women's groups hoped to reshape them. The "problem," if one existed, was that women's and men's interests varied by the time they got to Brown. Testifying for the defense, renowned statistician Finis Welch said that while the athletic interests of pre-adolescent and early adolescent boys and girls are similar, "By the time men and women reach college their respective interests and abilities in participating in intercollegiate athletics are different."[8]

"We kept trying to show that if you take a high school population that doesn't have anything to do with Brown you get the same disparity," says Ledbetter. "You look at the group that sent Brown its data—same thing. You look at the group that applied to Brown— same thing. Where do you then get this 50/50 [mandated participation ratio]? Or 51/49? There wasn't any data or factual support for this proposition, much less for this conclusion."

Then, in what many courtroom observers considered a *coup de grâce,* Michaelson and Connolly presented the compelling fact that at the time the lawsuit was filed, Brown's men's teams were forced to turn away would-be participants while almost all of its women's teams had room for additional players. In fact, there were 93 unfilled slots on women's varsity teams at the time Amy Cohen charged discrimination against women—opportunities to play that, for whatever reason, went unrealized by Brown women. If these unfilled spots on women's teams were counted toward the gender quota, the Brown defense calculated, their "Title IX gap" virtually disappeared. How, then, could the university be accused of failing to "accommodate" Brown women's athletic interests and abilities?

As for Amy Cohen and her teammates, who had demonstrated an interest in specific sports but had their opportunities to play limited, the Brown defense team argued that the law didn't obligate the university to satisfy every single woman who wanted to play a particular sport. Rather, it required that Brown equally accommodate the interests of both men and women to the degree they could. Not all students of either sex who want to be athletes will be able to play sports, they argued. And if there are differing levels of interest between the sexes, the law allows a school to take that into account when rationing scarce opportunities.

"You cannot look at interest *in vacuo;* you have to look at males and females together," said Connolly. "All of the burden of Brown's budgetary constraints have been foisted on the men's teams to this date. Six men's club teams cry out to participate [at the varsity level]."[9] But these men were denied the opportunity to play sports, not because there were so many women clamoring for a place on a varsity squad, but because the current enforcement of the law put a ceiling on men's participation.

"We have arrived at a truly absurd state of affairs," wrote Brown's athletic director David Roach in the *Washington Post*.

> It no longer matters whether a college gives men and women absolutely equal opportunities to play varsity sports. Equal opportunity is not what the compliance test measures. Instead, the test determines whether the college can manipulate its athletic program so that men and women appear to participate in equal numbers regardless of their interest and ability to participate.
>
> In fact—and here's where things get almost too absurd—if a school has equal numbers of men and women in its student body and gives all interested male and female athletes a scrupulously equal chance at participating on varsity teams, that school will almost certainly fail the government's Title IX compliance test. We aren't in Kansas anymore.[10]

ON MARCH 29, 1995, Judge Pettine found for Amy Cohen and the other female athletes. Brown promptly appealed and then, in January 1996—ten months before the appeals court ruled—Amy Cohen's lawyers received some help from a welcome source: Clinton administration Office for Civil Rights head Norma Cantu. OCR, which hadn't previously taken a position in the Brown case, suddenly issued a "clarification" of the 1979 Policy Interpretation—ostensibly to provide struggling colleges and universities with clearer guidance on how to comply with Title IX in athletics.

Although the OCR's directive purported to be a simple restatement of the three-part test, both its timing and pointed changes in wording seemed designed to help Amy Cohen prevail in her case. The crucial change came in the new interpretation of the third part of the three-part test: whether the athletic interests of women are accommodated by the current program. OCR manuals for Title IX investigators written in 1980 and 1990—the most recent instances in which OCR had commented formally on Title IX—directed federal officials to consider whether the interests of *both* sexes were "equally and effectively accommodated." Schools are required, read the 1980 investigators' manual, only to "meet the interests and abilities of women to the same degree as they meet the interests and abilities of men." The 1990 manual instructed investigators to determine "whether the current program *equally effectively accommodates the interests and abilities of male and female athletes*" (emphasis added).[11]

But just like Amy Cohen's lawyers, the new OCR directive decreed that the interests of only the "underrepresented sex" be "*fully* and effectively accommodated" (emphasis added). And lest the court miss the message implicit in the change in wording, the OCR document contained the following warning, aimed, it seemed, directly at Brown: "If an institution has recently eliminated a viable team from the intercollegiate program, OCR will find that there is sufficient interest, ability and available competition to sustain an intercollegiate team in that sport."

OCR's new "interpretation" so alarmed higher education that sixty other colleges and universities joined Brown in arguing that the move "changed the meaning of Title IX in a way contrary to the express language of the statute." The new enforcement regime, they argued, established an "irrebuttable presumption of compliance" with Title IX only in statistical proportionality. If—and only if—schools achieve proportionality are they immune to legal challenge and federal investigation. Otherwise, the "underrepresented sex" must be "fully" accommodated until it is no longer underrepresented. That is, until the sex quota is filled.

The Brown defense suspected that the new OCR directive was designed not just to codify the arguments advanced by the plaintiffs, but to send a message to the appeals court as well. And sure enough, on November 21, 1996, a three-judge panel of the U.S. Court of Appeals for the First Circuit affirmed Judge Pettine's lower court ruling against Brown. The university, it said, had discriminated against Amy Cohen and her teammates in violation of Title IX by demoting their teams in 1991. The opinion gave full deference to OCR's judgments, both the 1979 Policy Interpretation and the 1996 reinterpretation, as it shot down Brown's reading of the three-part test.

The first test, proportionality, the opinion read, "is merely the starting point for analysis, rather than the conclusion; a rebuttable presumption, rather than an inflexible requirement." Brown, however, had failed to "rebut" the presumption of discrimination attached to its failure of the proportionality test. Furthermore, the court ruled, the university could not show a "history and continuing practice of program expansion" of women's athletics under the second test. And as for the third test, allowing Brown to have fewer female athletes because fewer women were interested—the defense team's last, best resort—the court shot it down emphatically, and broke new legal ground in doing so:

"We view Brown's argument that women are less interested than men in participating in intercollegiate athletics, as well as its conclusion that institutions should be required to accommodate the interests and abilities of its female students only to the extent that it accommodates the interests and abilities of its male students, with great suspicion," the First Circuit wrote. "Even if it can be empirically demonstrated that, at a particular time, women have less interest in sports than do men, such evidence, standing alone, cannot justify providing fewer athletic opportunities for women than men" because women's lesser demonstrated interest in sports is strictly the result of "women's historical lack of opportunities to participate in sports."

It was back to "if you build it, they will come." Title IX, in the eyes of the court, made the question of differing interests between men and women that Brown had labored to demonstrate at trial utterly irrelevant. The law created the responsibility for Brown not simply to respond to women's athletic interest, but to *create* it through a sort of athletic remediation, ruled the First Circuit.

> Interest and ability rarely develop in a vacuum; they evolve as a function of opportunity and experience. The Policy Interpretation recognizes that women's lower rate of participation in athletics reflects women's historical lack of opportunities to participate in sports. To allow a numbers-based lack-of-interest defense to become the instrument of further discrimination against the underrepresented gender would pervert the remedial purpose of Title IX.

So there it was. Twenty-four years after the passage of the law, the court had discovered a "remedial" purpose to Title IX. Even as the California voters who supported Proposition 209 and the Fifth Circuit Court of Appeals in Texas were in the process of outlawing remedial affirmative action on the basis of race, the court in *Brown v. Cohen* was mandating affirmative action on the basis of sex under Title IX. Not only that, but the federal Office for Civil Rights had made the decision of the First Circuit the law of the land in all fifty states.

Casper Weinberger, the author of the original Title IX regulations as secretary of Health, Education and Welfare in 1975, called the decision "flatly contrary to the HEW regulations." Both the statute and the original regulation, said Weinberger, "make clear that Title IX does not require a school either to ignore the actual interests of its students...or to take affirmative action simply for the purpose of equalizing the number of men and women participating in particular programs." And testifying before the House Subcommittee on Postsecondary Education in 1995, Brown University president Vartan Gregorian railed against what he called an "arbitrary numerical reference system."

"I am a frustrated university administrator who does not like bureaucracy and who does not like to be intimidated by lawyers and who would like a clear policy," Gregorian told the lawmakers. "I cannot tell these women, 'You better participate in athletics, otherwise you cause problems.' It's a Catch-22. If you create a team and don't have participation you're held accountable. If you don't have the team you're held accountable on opportunity."[12]

In addition to Gregorian, the hearing, called by the newly Republican-dominated House of Representatives in the aftermath of the First Circuit's ruling, featured a parade of athletes and coaches who complained that Title IX had led to cuts in men's programs and little or no new opportunity for women. Congressman and former wrestling coach Dennis Hastert expressed support for Title IX but regret for its "unintentional consequence." No member of Congress suggested amending Title IX or weakening its commitment to equal opportunity for women. Still, the hearing was savaged in the press as a conspiracy of the Republican-controlled Congress and big-time football to "gut" Title IX. For critics of gender quotas, things did not look good. But Brown had one final appeal.

"THE MOST COMMON REASON for the Supreme Court to take a case is if there is a conflict in the circuits," says Washington lawyer Maureen Mahoney. "But we couldn't pretend there was a split in the district courts."

In fact, when Mahoney filed Brown's petition for writ of certiorari from the Supreme Court in February 1997, asking the high court to review their case, the district courts were unanimous. In the months since Brown had suffered its defeat, every circuit court of appeals to address the issue had reached the same conclusion. The Third, Sixth, Seventh and Tenth Circuit Courts had followed suit and adopted the *Cohen* interpretation of Title IX enforcement. Gender quotas in athletics, it seemed, were fast on their way to becoming a fact of American life.

Forced to work with what they had, Mahoney and the rest of Brown's legal team argued that it was this prospect—that the First Circuit's decision was being echoed in other circuits and had been given national scope by the OCR reinterpretation—that warranted Supreme Court review of the case. The new Title IX interpretation, they argued, would not be confined to the First Circuit but would be binding on *all* schools across the country unless the high court ruled. What's more, the First Circuit's decision contradicted not just the words of the statute, but also the history of Supreme Court jurisprudence on civil rights.

Brown's petition to the Supreme Court pointed to the language of Title IX expressly *not* requiring "preferential treatment" for one sex based on its lack of representation in an educational program, and argued that it mirrored, almost word for word, language in Title VII of the 1964 Civil Rights Act outlawing discrimination in employment.

"What we know about Title IX is, just like Title VII, it's supposed to guarantee equal opportunity," says Maureen Mahoney. "It says schools are not supposed to grant preferences based on someone's sex. But that is the inevitable result of using a rule in athletics that says participation should be fifty-fifty unless and until there is equal interest." The *Cohen* decision places an unreasonable burden on colleges and universities, Mahoney argues.

> I'm not rooting against there being equal interest and I don't think most people are. The issue is: who is responsible for the level of interest? Are schools supposed to artificially create programs in order to generate and increase interest or are they supposed to respond to the pool that is out there? It's quite clear under Title VII and it should be quite clear under any equal opportunity statute that you must respond to the pool that is out there, that you're not responsible for reforming the world.

Brown asserted in its appeal that the Supreme Court had agreed with this argument before. In *Wards Cove Packing Co. v. Antonio,* a group of Filipino cannery workers filed an employment discrimination suit against a fish packing plant in Alaska alleging that they were being singled out for lower-paying, unskilled jobs because of their race. The cannery workers argued successfully in a lower court that they had been discriminated against because although the local community was 90 percent white, the people laboring in the lower-paying cannery jobs were 80 percent Filipino. The Supreme Court, however, overturned the decision, ruling that the appropriate standard of comparison for determining whether the cannery workers were being discriminated against wasn't all the citizens of the local community, but just those qualified for the unskilled jobs. The fact that the percentage of Filipinos in these jobs failed to match the percentage of Filipinos in the community, the Court ruled, did not constitute a prima facie case of employment discrimination under Title VII.

The Brown defendants, in making their case for Supreme Court review, contended that this "qualified pool" analysis also applied to sex discrimination under Title IX. As in the *Wards Cove* case, they argued, the appropriate standard of comparison for judging whether there was discrimination against women in Brown athletics wasn't the number of female athletes versus the total number of women at Brown, but the number of female athletes versus the pool of women interested in varsity sports and capable of competing. Says Mahoney:

> The First Circuit never really confronts this. They can't. What they say instead is that we think that Title IX was supposed to help remedy the situation. But that begs the question of what "situation" Title IX was designed to help remedy. If you sued a school and showed that they had a history of intentional discrimination which caused them to have an athletic program that is three-quarters male but it's quite clear from their applicant pool that there's a lot more women's interest than that—they certainly can be required to remedy that by adding teams or doing something under Title IX. But what you can't do is to require an institution—whether it's a school or an employer—to remedy societal discrimination. That's what the First Circuit ordered in *Cohen* and they understood that's what they were ordering.

Brown was joined by fifty colleges and universities, former HEW secretary Casper Weinberger, the College Football Association, the governing bodies of intercollegiate wrestling, swimming and water polo, the American Council on Education, forty-eight members of the House of Representatives and one senator in its appeal to the Supreme Court to overturn the First Circuit's opinion in *Cohen*. The Clinton administration Department of Justice joined Amy Cohen in arguing that the Supreme Court should allow the First Circuit's ruling to stand. Writing for the administration, the assistant attorney general for civil rights, Deval Patrick, approvingly quoted selections of the First Circuit's ruling decreeing that Title IX's purpose is not to deter discrimination, but to remedy past injustice. The court, Patrick wrote, "correctly held that the Department of Education's Title IX regulations are entitled to deference"—including the OCR "guidance" issued in the middle of the litigation.

Patrick also addressed Brown's "qualified pool" analysis of Title IX compliance. This interpretation, he wrote, "undercuts the fundamental framework of Title IX."

"Job opportunities, unlike competitive sports, are not segregated by sex," wrote Patrick. "The sex separation of sports teams creates the risk that the smaller overall size of the program designated for women will have the effect of discouraging women from participating in sports." Echoing the Cohen legal team almost word for word, Patrick laid out the "field of dreams" argument for the justices: "Team size is largely predetermined by the institution's own recruiting practices. This typically gives rise to recruiting only enough women to fill spaces in a program that underrepresents women, thus leaving the institution to defend that underrepresentation based on the level of interest of its recruits."

The Brown legal team's rejoinder was that, yes, you do have to take sex into account in recruiting athletes and funding athletic opportunities for sex-segregated teams. You also have to take sex into account in building sex-segregated housing on campus. But the Title IX regulations state explicitly that schools are to determine the extent of their single-sex housing on the basis of interest, not a numerical formula.

"What it says in the Title IX regulations quite clearly is you look at the total pool of interested students and if there is a higher percentage of women interested in living in college dorms then a higher percentage of the dorms will be allocated to women," says Mahoney. "It doesn't say that if you have male dorms and female dorms that you need to make sure you have 50 percent of the dorm rooms for women and 50 percent of the dorm rooms for men."

So where are the lawsuits clamoring for "gender equity" in campus housing? Mahoney explains,

> There is a normative judgment going on here that underlies this whole thing. Some people have gotten together and decided that we think men and women *should* be equally interested in sports and therefore participation has to be fifty-fifty. But when you look at the housing situation you don't see universities saying, "We think men and women *should* be equally interested in living in campus dorms." What's different here is women have decided that men and women *should* be equally interested in varsity athletics. But as a normative matter, why should we think that? Why should

we prefer that women play soccer as opposed to live in a dorm or dance ballet?

BEFORE IT WAS OVER, THE Brown case went through four separate lower court rulings spanning fifty-three months at a cost to the university that soared into the millions. Then, on April 21, 1997, the Supreme Court announced that it would not review the First Circuit's ruling. As usual, no explanation was given for the decision, no clue as to why the Court refused either to affirm or to overturn the ruling of the lower court. *Cohen v. Brown* was allowed to stand.

"Absent somebody deciding they want to spend the enormous sums required to amass statistical evidence, the message of this case is loud and clear," said the victorious Arthur Bryant of Trial Lawyers for Public Justice. "Don't waste money on studies. Spend it on athletics."[13]

In a technical legal sense, Bryant is wrong. The *Cohen* decision is binding only for the states and territories that fall under the First Circuit Court's jurisdiction: Massachusetts, Rhode Island, Maine, New Hampshire and Puerto Rico. For this reason, Maureen Mahoney believes that sex quotas under Title IX are not yet settled law.

"Schools shouldn't give up on this issue," Mahoney says. "There are lots of schools operating within jurisdictions where there is no binding precedent. And when you look at the numbers it's really stark in terms of what this interpretation means for the future. [Schools] will either have to cut thousands of men or add thousands of women's positions. They should feel free to litigate within their own jurisdictions."

But so far, this message appears not to have penetrated the ranks of American colleges and universities. In fact, the Brown decision has had a powerful chilling effect on male athletes who have had their sports careers ended in the name of "gender equity." The overwhelming majority of the estimated twenty thousand athletes whose teams have been cut to meet Title IX quotas have either accepted their fate or sought to salvage what they can of their collegiate athletic careers by transferring to other schools. A very few have attempted to mount Title IX reverse discrimination cases against the schools that dismissed them. And those who have attempted to fight back in the courts, so far, have been uniformly unsuccessful.

One short-lived exception was four-time All-American and Academic All-American wrestler Stephen Neal of the California State University at Bakersfield (CSUB). Under court-ordered pressure to achieve proportionality in its athletic program by 1998, Cal State Bakersfield ran up against a big roadblock in 1997: Its largely commuter student body was a full 64 percent female but its athletic program was stubbornly stuck at 39 percent female, despite offering more women's teams than men's. Neal's coach, T. J. Kerr, fought a creative battle to protect his squad from Title IX cuts, at one point declaring his wrestling squad coed and encouraging Bakersfield women to try out. To make it appear that more women were playing sports, CSUB first tried capping the wrestling squad, forcing Kerr to cut ten men from the team. Then, when the administration threatened to cut the team altogether, Neal and his teammates—including eight female wrestlers—went to court. The cuts, they challenged, represented discrimination on the basis of sex in violation of Title IX.

In the lone court decision in the history of the statute prohibiting the elimination of men's sports opportunities under Title IX, U.S. district court judge Robert E. Coyle agreed with Neal. Bakersfield, he ordered, was forbidden to make additional cuts to its wrestling program in the name of "gender equity" on the grounds that the proportionality test was "inconsistent with the text, structure and policy of Title IX itself." But in December 1999—the same month the Seventh Circuit Court in Chicago dashed the hopes of a group of wrestlers and male soccer players who sued the University of Illinois for reverse discrimination under Title IX when their programs were axed—a three-judge panel of the U.S. Court of Appeals for the Ninth Circuit reversed Neal's victory.

The *Cohen* case, said the Ninth Circuit, had established that a "central aspect of Title IX's purpose was to encourage women to participate in sports." "Remedial actions" for women—and discrimination against men—were therefore justified because "the increased number of roster spots and scholarships reserved for women would gradually increase demand among women." Although the three-judge panel failed to say how lessening opportunities for men increases the roster spots or scholarship opportunities for women, its opinion is a candid, if depressing, description of the philosophy underlying current Title IX enforcement: if you build it, they will come.

Rejecting any pretense that Title IX is intended to level the playing field, the Ninth Circuit opinion quotes a *Harvard Law Review* article entitled "Cheering on Women and Girls: Using Title IX to Fight Gender Role Oppression" to say what most OCR officials and women's activists will not admit, at least in public: "In effect, the 'substantially proportionate' approach recognizes that women's attitudes toward sports are socially constructed and have been limited by discrimination and gender stereotypes. Congress passed Title IX to combat such discrimination and stereotypes, thereby changing the social environment in which girls and women develop, or do not develop, interests in sports."

Thus had social constructionism, a cliché of the postmodern university, come home to roost in the law and in college sports.

"THE BROWN DECISION WAS LIKE a 2-by-4 to the head of all those people who refused to comply with the law," says Amy Cohen's attorney, Lynette Labinger. Indeed, the standard of Title IX compliance established by the *Cohen* decision—and its codification in federal policy with the 1996 OCR policy reinterpretation—has had its intended effect: to intimidate colleges and universities into establishing gender quotas in their athletic programs. Since the women's gymnastics and volleyball teams were demoted at Brown in 1991, no NCAA Division I college or university has dropped a women's team. The University of Washington briefly considered doing away with its women's swimming team in the summer of 2000, but the ensuing outcry led university officials to reverse their decision.

As a slowing economy forces administrators to tighten belts, some colleges are coming to regret the rapid, arbitrary expansion of women's programs forced by Title IX. But now that the landscape is littered with struggling women's water polo and synchronized swimming teams, getting rid of them is impossible. "I've heard lots of people say, 'We never should have started so-and-so sport,' but I've never heard anyone talking about dropping a sport" for women, said University of Virginia athletic director M. Terry Holland. "With the Brown decision, that said to me, 'Don't drop women's sports unless you are in compliance.' "[14]

Still, for many schools, not dropping women's teams or even adding women's teams won't get them to the "safe harbor" of substantial proportionality. Men's opportunities in most cases must be limited by capping squad sizes or by eliminating whole teams. Even before the Supreme Court ruled, Brown reached a settlement with Judge Pettine that committed the school to Title IX quotas for female athletes within 3.5 percent of their representation in the student body. Women's water polo, gymnastics, fencing and skiing were guaranteed funding, regardless of student interest. And if Brown eliminated a women's sport or attempted to create a men's varsity squad without creating a corresponding women's team, it would be penalized by a quota for women that increased to within 2.25 percent of the female share of the student body.

Following the decision, the *Chronicle of Higher Education* reported that the new teams were having trouble attracting female athletes at Brown, and the settlement with the court left a residue of mixed feelings among the female athletes it was supposed to benefit. "Last year, we had to add players—walk-ons—just to fill slots, while the men's lacrosse team had to cut players to make up for it," said Leyla Goldsmith, captain of the downgraded volleyball team. "That was completely unfair."[15]

Meanwhile, although no teams have been eliminated, men's positions at Brown have been cut to stay within the court-ordered participation ratio. For the first time in his twenty-eight years of coaching the men's cross-country team, Bob Rothenberg has been forced to turn away walk-ons. Under the quota, Rothenberg is allowed to add one male runner over the maximum limit on the men's squad only if he can recruit two women over the minimum number mandated on the women's team.

It is telling that although the trial lawyers and women's groups who brought the Brown case claimed publicly to be seeking justice for the female athletes whose teams had been demoted, only one of those teams, the gymnastics squad, was resurrected in the court-mandated settlement. The volleyball team was never refunded. "In my view, they won a battle and lost a war," says Brown counsel Beverly Ledbetter. "They beat Brown, but what has happened as a consequence is that men's teams have been cut, not women's teams significantly added."

Over a decade after Amy Cohen first brought her lawsuit, bitter feelings linger at Brown University. "Brown was doing the right thing. It was doing the equitable thing. It was doing the morally appropriate, the correct thing," Ledbetter says of the school's philosophy on athletic participation. "And this was an outrageous reading of the law."

FOUR

PLAYING DOCTOR WITH THE LAW: TITLE IX AND SEXUAL HARASSMENT

As the century draws to a close, it appears that the
campaign against sexual harassment may, in fact, be the
success story of twentieth-century feminism.
———Jane Gallop, *Feminist Accused*

FOR THIRTY YEARS, MARY DALY preached her own particular brand of "radical-lesbian-feminist ethics" at Jesuit-run Boston College. There was the occasional dust-up on campus over her frequent jihads against the "phallocracy," but for the most part BC tolerated Daly in silence. The Roman Catholic university averted its eyes when Daly advocated the abolition of "patriarchal religions" such as Catholicism on the ground that their male-dominated structures are abusive to women. After BC began to admit women in 1970, officials also looked the other way when she declared her classroom off-limits to men. A women-only classroom environment, Daly proclaimed, created a "safe space" for women to learn, which fostered a special kind of creative energy that she liked to call "gynergy."

But finally in 1999, Boston College lost its patience with Mary Daly. The last straw wasn't ideological or even theological; it was legal. Duane Naquin, a BC senior who had been denied entry to Daly's "Introduction to Feminist Ethics I" class (which examined "the interconnected atrocities perpetuated against women and nature in patriarchal society"), threatened to sue. With the help of the Center for Individual Rights, a conservative public interest law firm based in Washington, D.C., Naquin charged that Daly's exclusion of men was illegal under Title IX. While the law permits single-sex institutions to have single-sex classes, he claimed, a professor at a coed school can't simply decide to exclude men—however they might effect the "gynergy" in the room. Naquin presented BC with an ultimatum: get him into Mary Daly's class, or he would take them to court.

Boston College took Naquin's threat seriously. In the spring of 1999 the BC administration asked Daly to either admit men to her class or resign. She refused to do either, promptly went on sabbatical and insisted she still had a job. When she returned in the fall of 1999, with a camera crew in tow, to the campus office she had occupied for thirty-three years, preparations had already begun for the next occupant. The walls were freshly spackled and painted. Daly's possessions lay in a heap in the center of the room. Copies of her books, *Pure Lust* and *Outercourse,* littered the floor.

Daly was out, but she refused to go quietly. With her attorney, feminist lawyer Gretchen Van Ness, Daly countersued the university. Boston College, she charged, was "caving in to right-wing pressure and depriving me of my right to teach freely." Her dismissal for not allowing men into her classroom wasn't about fairness but "about leveling the rights of women and minorities so that white male power reigns."

"I'm a radical lesbian," Daly said on National Public Radio, "and it scares them."

For all the rhetoric of female empowerment that characterized her career, Daly's legal case was based on the need for women to be protected from victimization at the hands of men—a protection, she argued, that was granted by Title IX. "We've seized this space on the boundary of a patriarchal institution," she said.[1] "Women in classes with men...have to be sexy and they can't really think," she told NPR. "One quiet little fellow with a beard, that would do it. It would stop discussion."

Daly's attorney declared that their creative use of a law that bans discrimination on the basis of sex to justify discrimination against men was "the cutting edge of Title IX." Daly could exclude men from her classes, Van Ness maintained, because the law "recognizes that in some circumstances it is not discriminatory to treat men and women differently—to remedy past discrimination, to create more opportunities for women, to serve a valid educational goal." Van Ness told the *New York Times* that Title IX was meant to combat stereotypical views of women such as that they "can't play sports." But Daly, she said, "came to decide to teach the way she teaches not based on stereotypes or intentional discrimination but on her very, very real experience of what it meant for her students for her to teach in a mixed class rather than separate classes."[2] In other words, Dr. Daly's view of women as victims was based on "real experience," not some outdated stereotype.

In February 2001, the day before her case was to go to court, Mary Daly reached a settlement with Boston College under still undisclosed terms. She agreed not to contest her retirement from the college and not to say anything more. But, true to form, attorney Van Ness the next day issued a press release (which she was later forced to retract) declaring the settlement a "victory" for Daly. In a very real sense, the lawyer was right. For twenty-five years, in violation of the letter and original intent of Title IX, Daly had excluded men from her classroom at a coeducational college. Although her attempt to use the same law to defend her discrimination against men was never tested in court, she was supported by feminist icons such as Gloria Steinem and Eleanor Smeal. Academic organizations like the American Association of University Professors rallied to her cause. Daly now tours college campuses, drawing enthusiastic audiences to hear her rail against the higher education patriarchy that "trampled on" her academic freedom to give women their own "creative space."

Daly's case is perhaps an extreme one. With the notable exception of athletic departments, few in education have her chutzpa to actively exclude boys and men from programs in the name of "gender equity." But in a lengthening list of other areas of education, from testing to math and science classes to the accommodation of pregnant students, Title IX is being used to carve out a "protected space" for women—at the expense of men. For all her celebrity as a pioneer in the "radical feminist" movement, Mary Daly was not really a trailblazer. She was merely following what was, by the late 1990s, a well-trod path of Title IX out of the world of sports and into the classrooms and hallways of academia.

THE SAME CONVERGENCE OF events that sparked the surge in Title IX enforcement activity in sports in the early 1990s also initiated the expansion of the law as a gender preference regime into other areas of education. The availability of money damages after the *Franklin* decision and the feminist advocates throughout the Clinton administration awakened supporters of proportionality to the possibility that the quest for "gender equity" need not stop at the locker room. By 1995, the *New York Times* reported triumphantly that "in the last three years, the use of Title IX has moved well beyond the playing field, expanding slowly but surely into a legal tool that touches on the most delicate areas of student-to-student, or teacher-student, relationships."

"It's like that ad, 'It's not just for breakfast anymore,'" crowed Verna Williams, senior counsel for the National Women's Law Center. "Title IX's not just sports anymore. It's a tool for making schools more hospitable for girls and women, ending sexual harassment, and winning real gender equity across the board in education."[3]

For gender feminists like Williams, the expansion of Title IX came not a moment too soon. The growing presence of girls and women in athletics—as well as their increasingly well-publicized exploits there—threatened to create the impression that things were actually getting better for women. By 1999, the bright, shining success story of women's soccer, and its linkage to Title IX in the media, had come back to haunt those women's activists whose livelihoods depend on the perception of persistent and systemic sexism in America's schools. And they didn't like it one bit. "The focus on women's sports feeds a wide misperception that we, as a nation, have achieved the goal of Title IX and that our educational institutions are gender-fair," reads a 2000 report from the American Association of University Women (AAUW). "Far from it."

At the top of the women's groups' list of gender inequities still thriving in American schools is sexual harassment. To commemorate the twenty-fifth anniversary of the passage of Title IX, the National Coalition of Women and Girls in Education (NCWGE), a consortium of liberal education, women's and legal groups, issued a "Title IX report card." This publicity stunt had two goals: to remind the country of the vast expanse of educational territory that falls under the jurisdiction of Title IX, and to express the belief that the law is woefully underutilized. "If the Title IX report card could send but one message to the American public—hands down—it would be that this law is about much more than college athletics," said Janice Weinman, the executive director of the AAUW. "To focus exclusively on the glamour of sports ignores Title IX's far-reaching impact on educational opportunity off the playing field."

Predictably, in no area of education covered by the report—rooting out gender bias in testing, providing access to math and science courses and many others—did Title IX receive a higher grade than a B-minus (for access to higher education—at a time when women are surpassing men as undergraduates!). On leveling the playing field in athletics, the law rated a gentleman's C. And on the struggle to end sexual harassment, Title IX all but flunked. Signaling its priority to turn the "hostile hallways" of America's schools into safer places for girls and women, the NCWGE gave enforcement of sexual harassment law the lowest grade on the Title IX report card, a D-plus.

Title IX sexual harassment cases exploded in the 1990s, not just because the *Franklin* decision made them a lucrative enterprise for trial lawyers, but because, thanks to groups like the NCWGE, the definition of the offense was expanding rapidly. Today, a vast and still growing range of behavior is covered under the definition of sexual harassment in schools. The Office for Civil Rights classifies any and all of the following as illegal harassment under Title IX:

- sexual advances
- touching of a sexual nature
- graffiti of a sexual nature
- displaying or distributing sexually explicit drawings, pictures or written materials
- sexual gestures or sexual jokes
- pressure for sexual favors
- touching oneself sexually or talking about one's sexual activity in front of others
- spreading rumors about or rating other students' sexual activity or performance

The American Association of University Women, a powerful interest group in the campaign for expanding Title IX enforcement, goes so far as to make the victim herself the arbiter of what is or is not sexual harassment. " 'Unwelcomeness' is the determining factor in assessing whether a sexual behavior is considered sexual harassment," says a 2000 AAUW report.[4] The leading guide for colleges and universities in ferreting out harassers, *Sexual Harassment on Campus: A Guide for Administrators, Faculty, and Students* (edited by Bernice R. Sandler, perhaps the founding mother of Title IX) provides a list of slights that includes "humor or jokes about sex or females in general," "touching a person," "calling women hot stuff, cutiepie, etc." and "laughing or not taking seriously someone who experiences sexual harassment."

Most Americans could be forgiven for not immediately understanding why sexual harassment is covered by an anti–sex discrimination law like Title IX. That's because they still hold to the traditional understanding of sexual harassment as a crime against an individual, not an act of discrimination against an entire group.

Many of us still think of sexual harassment as what is known today as merely one subcategory of harassment, "quid pro quo" harassment. This is usually a demand for sexual favors by a person in a position of power, which, if not met, has negative consequences for the person (usually a woman) of lesser power. In a school setting, this would typically be a teacher or professor demanding sex from a student in return for grades or promotion.

The definitions of sexual harassment promulgated by the OCR and the AAUW, of course, go much further than this. They are part of a second type of harassment, called "hostile environment" harassment, which involves touches, words and even looks of a sexual nature that have "the purpose of…creating an intimidating, hostile or offensive work environment."

How did sexual harassment of an individual, however egregious, become prosecutable under Title IX, a law that outlaws "discrimination on the basis of sex"? How did telling dirty jokes, calling a woman "hot stuff" or even threatening retaliation for failing to get a date become discrimination against an entire class of people? After all, as legal writer Jeffrey Rosen points out, "Desire may be rampant, but it is not general. A man does not hit on a gender."

That legal leap is widely credited to one woman: feminist legal theorist Catherine MacKinnon. In her 1979 book, *The Sexual Harassment of Working Women*, MacKinnon laid the philosophical foundation for interpreting sexual harassment as discrimination by arguing that men and women are defined first and foremost by their sex. To MacKinnon, we are not the sum of our unique choices and individual traits, but prisoners of our gender. "Male and female are created through the eroticization of dominance and submission. The man/woman difference and the dominance/submission dynamic define each other," MacKinnon contends. The sex act, then, is the ultimate act of female victimization. "The male sexual role centers on aggressive intrusion on those with less power," and thus does our basic sexuality itself beget "a theory of gender inequality, meaning the social hierarchy of men over women."

In the MacKinnonite view, sexual harassment is not simply the result of a few dirty old men in positions of power, but the inevitable consequence of the structure of American society—a structure in which women, by their nature, are held to an inferior and subordinate role. Since the sexes are unequal, "practices which express and reinforce the social inequality of women to men are clear cases of sex-based discrimination." Sexual harassment, MacKinnon famously wrote, "eroticizes women's subordination. It acts out and deepens the powerlessness of women as a gender, *as women.*" According to MacKinnon, to be hit on is to be feminized. And to be feminized is to be subordinated.

In the hypertrophied climate of the early 1990s, MacKinnon's ideas spread like a contagion from the politically correct university into the workplace, where they soon inspired sexual harassment cases. Instances of alleged sex discrimination in employment typically do not fall under Title IX (except in some cases involving employees of schools and universities) but under Title VII of the Civil Rights Act, which outlaws discrimination in employment, including discrimination based on sex. By 1986 the Supreme Court had established not only that sexual harassment in employment was actionable under Title VII, but that what constituted sexual harassment was vastly expanded under the MacKinnon-inspired "hostile environment" standard. A woman's boss no longer had to retaliate against her for failure to comply with his amorous advances in order to be guilty of sexual harassment. All that was necessary now were words or looks deemed sufficiently offensive as to make a woman or a group of women feel disparaged. This new standard of harassment, which dispenses with the requirement that a woman actually suffer harm, is the apotheosis of the MacKinnonite vision. A woman now merely has to *perceive* harm and the consequence is that not only she but all women are damaged.

Just as it fails to mention sports, at no point does the Title IX statute mention sexual harassment. Nonetheless, the quid pro quo and hostile environment tests are now being zealously applied in Title IX school-based harassment claims. In the late 1990s, the courts, with the usual coordinated assistance from the Education Department's Office for Civil Rights, implemented the MacKinnonite worldview more thoroughly in policing sex relations in schools than in the workplace. In school-related Title IX cases, there need be no employer-employee imbalance of power and no threat of retaliation for sexual harassment to have occurred. Sexual harassment in schools is now something, in the words of MacKinnon, that "is done by men to women regardless of relative position on the formal hierarchy."[5] In schools today, the harasser can be a principal or a teacher, or more ominously, the little boy sitting two rows over.

The most important expansion of Title IX sexual harassment by the Supreme Court, in fact, came about because of a relationship between two ten-year-olds.

For months, LaShonda Davis was sexually taunted by a fifth-grade classmate at her school in Forsyth, Georgia. The boy, identified in court only as G.F., tried to grab LaShonda's breasts, rubbed against her in the hallways and whispered that he wanted to "get in bed" with her. He even put a doorstop in his pants and gestured with it suggestively. LaShonda's mother said she repeatedly asked school officials to intervene but nothing was done. So in 1994, after the boy had already pled guilty to sexual battery in state court, Davis sued the Monroe County School Board. Her child had been sexually harassed and the school had done nothing to protect her, the lawsuit charged. Therefore, the school district was guilty of discrimination under Title IX.

Until *Davis v. Monroe County Board of Education,* successful Title IX sexual harassment judgments were limited to students initiating actions against teachers, administrators and other employees of school districts. The reason was simple enough: sexual harassment law as it had evolved in the workplace does not impose liability on harassers but on those who employ them. Because employers exercise control over employees by hiring them and, if need be, firing them, the courts have concluded they can be held liable if they fail to exercise that control responsibly. A school district or a university, for example, that puts a teacher or professor in a position of authority over students and is deliberately indifferent to his harassing behavior can properly be held liable.

In the case of LaShonda Davis, however, the harasser was not an employee of the Monroe County School District, but a student—a student with a right, under the Georgia Constitution, to a free public education. In what sense could the school district be liable for G.F.'s actions? As attorneys for the school district pointed out in court, students can't be "fired" as teachers can. What's more, the harasser at issue was a child, whose behavior was much less controllable than an adult employee. Where does childish misbehavior and adolescent acting-out end and sexual harassment begin? Was G.F.'s pushing in the hallway a civil rights violation or just boorish, unsocialized behavior? And should courts and judges be meddling in disciplinary areas better suited to teachers and principals—or, better yet, to parents?

The question before the Supreme Court, in short, was whether Title IX should be expanded to impose a vast new potential liability on school districts, colleges and universities that federal law doesn't even impose on businesses: responsibility for the sexually tinged words, actions and looks of non-employees or "non-agents."

Sexual harassment attorney Jennifer Braceras, who wrote a brief in support of the Monroe County Schools for the Independent Women's Forum (IWF), argues that Title IX should not be expanded to encompass student-on-student harassment. "Because schools have an obligation to educate all students, and because students are more difficult to control than adult employees," says Braceras, "it strains logic to suggest that the failure of a school district to respond to a particular charge of student misconduct can constitute an act of intentional sex discrimination."

Braceras adds, "A kiss on the cheek, a sexually suggestive remark, the persistent pursuit of a romantic relationship with someone who is not interested, even unwanted sexual touching all may be normal parts of growing up when the individuals involved are peers. The same actions take on a decidedly different meaning when the perpetrator is a teacher and the target is a student."

And why single out behavior between students of different sexes? "On what basis should we treat inappropriate sexual behavior as more serious than other forms of student misconduct? Surely students who bring weapons to schools pose a far greater threat to our nation's students than preteens who tell dirty jokes," says Braceras. But if schools are made liable for student-on-student sexual harassment, they will be forced "to spend scarce resources conducting 'sexual harassment workshops' and disciplining students for handholding, rather than on implementing measures to keep guns out of schools."

Verna Williams of the National Women's Law Center presented the Davis family's argument before the Supreme Court. Aiding her case was the fact that the federal government had already opened the door to student-on-student sexual harassment actions under Title IX, in a "policy guidance" issued by the Office for Civil Rights two years earlier, warning that schools stood in danger of losing their federal funding if they failed to take action against peer harassment. The court, Williams argued, owed deference to the OCR policy and should find for LaShonda Davis.

The collaborative strategy of the OCR and the National Women's Law Center in *Davis,* critics charged, was troublingly reminiscent of how, in the midst of *Cohen v. Brown University,* the OCR suddenly issued new "policy guidance" that changed enforcement of the law to meet the plaintiff's standards. The Clinton OCR invented "peer harassment" liability for schools under Title IX in 1997 after the U.S. Court of Appeals for the Fifth Circuit rejected such a claim brought by two female eighth-graders who were tormented on their Texas school bus by several male classmates. The timing of the new OCR "guidance"—which appeared just in time for the Texas plaintiffs to cite it in their appeal to the Supreme Court—once again raised suspicions that OCR was engaged in a strategy of steering the courts to ever-expanding interpretations of Title IX.

The Monroe County legal team argued that the OCR sexual harassment policy guidance didn't merit the deference of the court because it "was adopted, not as a clarification of existing law, but rather, as a litigation strategy to push the courts into adopting a novel expansion of the law."[6] But when the Supreme Court ruled on the *Davis* case in May of 1999, it did in fact give deference to OCR's rendering of the law, and greatly expanded Title IX's scope in the hallways, playgrounds and classrooms of the nation's schools. The *Davis* ruling said that harassment like that suffered by LaShonda Davis at the hands of G.F. was actionable if it could be shown that officials exhibited "deliberate indifference" to the harassing behavior. The "deliberate indifference" caveat—reportedly inserted at the insistence of Justice Sandra Day O'Connor—afforded little comfort for schools worried about liability for students' actions. The Court had plunged the day-to-day teasing and taunting of schoolchildren into the murky waters of gender politics. O'Connor's attempt to contain the damage, wrote Justice Anthony Kennedy in a vigorous dissent for himself and Justices Rehnquist, Scalia and Thomas, would not succeed. The test that the majority claimed was narrow, he wrote, was, "in fact, so broad that it will support untold numbers of lawyers" and cause courts "to second-guess school administrators in every case."

Citing the case of Jonathan Prevette, the North Carolina six-year-old who was suspended from school for kissing a classmate on the cheek just weeks after OCR issued its revised sexual harassment "policy guidance," Kennedy predicted that "an avalanche of litigation" would hit schools as a result of the ruling. "The norms of the adult workplace that have defined hostile environment sexual harassment are not easily translated to peer relationships in schools," he wrote. "A teen-ager's romantic overtures to a classmate (even when persistent and unwelcome) are an inescapable part of adolescence." Trying to police them would create "a climate of fear that encourages school administrators to label even the most innocuous of childish conduct sexual harassment."

In fact, the climate of fear in the nation's schools was already well advanced by the time Kennedy wrote his dissent in *Davis*. Threatened with the loss of their federal funding by OCR's new sexual harassment policy, schools had begun to implement draconian sexual harassment regulations two years earlier. An Indiana elementary school issued a rule forbidding fourth-graders to hold hands, pass romantic notes or chase members of the opposite sex at recess. In Fullerton, California, the Nicolas Junior High School formally banned all public displays of affection, including hugging and kissing. Elsewhere, schools have instituted elaborate sexual harassment training programs and curricula. High-schoolers in Stevens Point, Wisconsin, put on a play called *Alice in Sexual Assault Land*. Minnesota's Board of Education approved a voluntary curriculum that uses puppets to explain sexual harassment to children in K–3. Kids in grades 4–6 get to analyze how television and advertising promote sex stereotypes and then write letters to the offenders

The *Davis* ruling merely ratcheted up the level of fear. Days after the Court spoke, a man who ran a federally funded welfare-to-work program for adults came into Jennifer Braceras's office to ask if *Davis* meant that he needed to kick out students who pursued romantic relationships with other students. Braceras said no, but the man said he probably would boot would-be Don Juans anyway, "just to be safe." Another client, representing a school board, asked if she should now mandate the separation of boys and girls on the school bus, where much allegedly harassing behavior takes place. "How ironic that the practical result of this 'feminist' victory is the segregation of the sexes!" says Braceras. "They've only just begun..."

IN JANUARY 2001, FOUR WEEKS before her case was scheduled to go to trial in federal court as the result of the Supreme Court ruling, LaShonda Davis reached a settlement with the Monroe County School District. Although the terms remain confidential, Davis reported she was "very pleased" with what she received. School officials would say only that they admitted no liability and that the case was "settled through our insurance company." Presumably, property taxes in Monroe County rose commensurate with the school district's premiums.

For most school administrators, the overriding lesson of the *Davis* decision has been to take steps to avoid liability of the kind Monroe

County refused to admit but nonetheless felt compelled to compensate LaShonda Davis for. As Daphne Patai writes in *Heterophobia,* a scathing criticism of sexual harassment politics in education today, schools have put in place a labyrinth of policies, training programs, sensitivity sessions and sexual harassment coordinators designed to cover their backsides. But according to Patai, this "Sexual Harassment Industry" in education has produced "not greater justice, not an absence of discrimination against women, but a climate that is inhospitable to all human beings."[7]

In March, the Sixth Circuit Court of Appeals in Cincinnati ruled that Macomb Community College has the right to suspend a professor for creating a "hostile learning environment" even if it means denying his right to free speech in the classroom. A female student filed a Title IX sexual harassment complaint against John C. Bonnell, an English professor, for using words like "damn," "ass" and "blow job" in class in reference to President Bill Clinton's affair with Monica Lewinsky. The student said that such language made her feel "degraded and sexually harassed." The college suspended Bonnell and he sued to be reinstated. But after Bonnell prevailed in a lower court, the Sixth Circuit ruled that his free speech took a back seat to the sensitivities of female students when gender politics were involved: "While a professor's rights to academic freedom and freedom of expression are paramount in the academic setting, they are not absolute to the point of compromising a student's right to learn in a hostile-free [*sic*] environment." Macomb Community College supported the ruling on the grounds that it helped "to provide and protect a nonhostile academic setting in which free expression and exchange of ideas thrives for both students and faculty."[8]

Bonnell and his lawyers argued that none of his statements in the classroom were ever directed at the student who filed the complaint, so he could not credibly be accused of discriminating against her. But in fact, OCR "guidelines" that determine what the federal government considers sexual harassment plainly state that "a hostile environment can occur even if harassment is not targeted specifically at the individual complainant." General statements directed at no one in particular, and damaging to no one in particular, can provoke a lawsuit, a federal investigation or, even more likely, preemptive penalties from skittish administrators.

It is this urge to act preemptively that has contributed to the transformation of university judicial boards into what one critic called "kangaroo courts, more interested in political correctness than guilt or innocence." The *Davis* decision opened the door to a lengthening list of sex crimes for students to accuse each other of—offenses ranging from date rape to the more amorphous charge of "unwanted sexual activity"—all included in the increasingly elastic definition of sexual harassment. Suddenly faced with liability for student-to-student sexual activity, university administrators are desperate for ways to settle sex-related complaints privately and quickly, before they reach federal courts or the OCR. Internal university judicial review boards offer a way out, but often at the expense of the due process rights of the accused.

A Massachusetts court set alarm bells ringing in the university community when it ruled that Brandeis University had violated the due process rights of junior David Schaer when a judicial review board found him guilty of "unwanted sexual activity" and creating "a hostile environment" for a woman who accused him of date rape. Schaer and the woman (whose name was never revealed by the university) agree on this much: They met in their sophomore year while working on the Brandeis student newspaper, ironically called *The Justice*. They dated, had sex once, and broke up. The next year, they ran into each other at a party. Later that night, both agree, the woman called Schaer and asked him if he wanted to come to her dorm to "fool around," by which, she acknowledges, she meant to have sex.

At this point, the encounter becomes the classic "he said / she said" tale of drunken collegiate sex. Schaer claims it was consensual. The woman claims she asked Schaer to stop and he didn't. In any case, the "trial" that ensued before the Brandeis Student Judicial Board didn't waste much time figuring out which one was telling the truth. The three-student, two-professor panel allowed the associate director of the Office of Student Life, who had initially approached Schaer to "talk" informally about the incident, to testify against him based on their conversation. A Brandeis police officer who didn't speak to the alleged victim until a month after the incident was allowed to testify that the woman "looked like a rape victim." Eleven other witnesses testified, but the official record, which only summarized Schaer's and his accuser's statements, is a mere twelve lines long.

Schaer was found guilty and suspended from Brandeis for the summer of 1996. Meanwhile, women's activists on campus, led by the Committee on Rape Education, conducted a campaign of vilification against him. Although the university had seen fit to convict him only of "unwanted sexual activity," Schaer was publicly tarred as a rapist. Petitions were circulated on campus calling for his expulsion. The dean of student affairs told him he was "damaged goods." When he had had enough, Schaer sued the university for failing to live up to its own judicial code. His hearing, he charged, had been a sham and a witch-hunt. Harvey Silverglate, a Boston civil rights lawyer who, along with the ACLU, supported Schaer, said that his case was not an isolated one: "The system has been perverted to accomplish preordained political goals. That is what makes this case important. It is really testing whether that can be done."[9]

A three-judge panel of the Massachusetts Court of Appeals found for Schaer in the fall of 1999, saying that Brandeis had trampled on due process rights spelled out in its own judicial code by failing to make an adequate record of the hearing and allowing "irrelevant and inflammatory evidence" to be introduced. But while Schaer and his supporters celebrated, higher education panicked. When Brandeis appealed the ruling to the Massachusetts Supreme Court, ten private colleges in the Boston area filed briefs in support. Their internal judicial boards would be overwhelmed with Title IX–inspired litigation, they warned, if the court ordered them to adhere to the same standards of due process observed in courtrooms outside the university. Better that they be allowed to dispense swift—if arbitrary—judgment of their own, especially when the alleged offense is sex-related.

In October 2000 the highest court in Massachusetts ruled that colleges and universities need not worry; Brandeis did not owe David Schaer the same protections he would receive in a criminal court. For Schaer's supporters, the ruling represented the continuation of a corrosive double standard in higher education: victims of Title IX–related sex offenses receive greater "justice" than others. "It was the date-rape charge that determined the case," said Harvey Silverglate. "Had this case involved a larceny by one student from another, and had there been a 12-line record of a 13-witness case, the ruling would have been 5-0 in the student's favor."[10]

The outrages of political correctness on college campuses are well known. But few of the critics of these excesses pause to consider the sources of university speech codes, policies and review boards that trample on the rights of students and the academic freedom of professors. It is true, of course, that universities today are breeding grounds for the excesses of identity politics. The motley crew of women's studies professors, queer theorists, racial essentialists and bored kids that can be found on most college campuses are capable of much mischief of their own. But risk-averse educational institutions are responding to outside pressures as well. And no law exerts more pressure on schools—and provides less instruction for its compliance—than Title IX. Colleges and universities are being asked to police the sexual behavior of young people in the prime of life and anything is fair game. Words, looks, gestures, pictures, feelings—all can be the basis for a lawsuit or a federal complaint. Under these conditions, it isn't merely to be expected that victims like David Schaer will be created; it is inevitable. And it is inevitable, too, that the universities will act before Title IX does.

THE FEMINISTS' FAVORITE STATISTIC for justifying more prosecution of Title IX sexual harassment is an oldie but goodie. It comes from a report produced in 1993 by the American Association of University Women called "Hostile Hallways," which disclosed the shocking statistic that 85 percent of girls had experienced sexual harassment in school (as well as an even more astonishing 76 percent of boys). Although the media uncritically reported this finding, scholars were skeptical—and rightly so. To arrive at this scarcely believable number, the AAUW had to define sexual harassment so broadly as to confuse—in the words of Al Shanker, the late president of the American Federation of Teachers—"acts that are criminal and acts that are merely rude."

Daphne Patai uses the term "domain expansion" to describe how Title IX sexual harassment cases, nonexistent twenty-five years ago, are pervasive today. Domain expansion is the process whereby once a problem has been identified, it provides the foundation for a whole new set of problems that are "essentially the same as" or "another form of" the original problem.

"At first we didn't have a word for it," says Title IX founding activist Bernice Sandler. "But when we had a word for it—'sexual harassment'—suddenly people had a label for behavior that they know about or have experienced." And what a difference a word makes. Under Title IX, old-fashioned quid pro quo harassment became "hostile environment" harassment, which in turn yielded "peer" harassment. Today the term sexual harassment encompasses virtually all aspects of behavior that can be said to have a sexual dimension, even if it is only in the eye of the beholder. And with each redefinition of the term, more and more of the meaning of Title IX as a tool to combat discrimination on the basis of sex has been lost.

Let me be clear: the indignities suffered by LaShonda Davis at the hands of G.F. were inexcusable, and the Monroe County School District had a moral obligation to see that they ended long before Davis's school finally took action. But it does not diminish the harm she suffered to recognize that it was not discrimination. What good can come, after all, from interjecting gender politics into the already difficult job of teachers and administrators struggling to maintain discipline in schools? Wouldn't it be a better use of the federal government's time and resources to see that existing policies designed to maintain order and civility in schools—regardless of the gender of the participants or the nature of their offense—be enforced?

The most recent expansion of Title IX to cases involving the alleged harassment of homosexuals does even greater damage to the original meaning of the law. In its sexual harassment policy guidance, issued in 1997, the Education Department's Office for Civil Rights brazenly declared same-sex harassment to be within its jurisdiction, even while acknowledging that it lies outside the scope of the law. "Although Title IX does not prohibit discrimination on the basis of sexual orientation," decreed the OCR, "sexual harassment directed at gay or lesbian students that is sufficiently serious to limit or deny a student's ability to participate in or benefit from the school's program constitutes sexual harassment prohibited by Title IX under the circumstances described in this guidance."

This statement was issued, as usual, in the middle of a high-profile harassment case in which the limits of the law were being tested. Jamie Nabozny was a gay high school junior in 1996 when he sued his school district in Ashland, Wisconsin. Nabozny claimed he was shoved, beaten, spat and urinated on by his classmates because he was gay. Repeated complaints to officials did nothing. His case in state court was thrown out, but a federal lawsuit filed with the help of the Lambda Legal Defense Fund, a gay and lesbian legal organization, bore fruit. A federal jury found the Ashland school administrators guilty of discrimination under Title IX. Nabozny received a nearly $1 million settlement from the school district, a victory that prompted similar lawsuits across the country. Today, Jamie Nabozny is a hero of the gay rights movement, and he tours the country speaking to high school students on gay issues.

The OCR policy statement including same-sex harassment under the umbrella of Title IX came after the Nabozny settlement, and just in time for Willi Wagner to pursue his Title IX sexual harassment case. Wagner was a high school junior who was fond of wearing painted two-inch nails and Egyptian pharaoh–style robes to his tenth-grade classes in Fayetteville, Arkansas. For this he was taunted mercilessly by his male classmates and at one point beaten so badly as to require hospitalization. Also with the help of the Lambda Legal Defense Fund, Wagner filed a complaint with the OCR in 1997 charging that what had happened to him was discrimination. OCR concurred and Wagner's school district was forced to settle. The district agreed to overhaul its policies on sexual harassment, train staff to ferret out same-sex harassment and spread the word that gays and lesbians are covered under Title IX.

Like other students, gay and lesbian students deserve a chance to learn. Cases of taunting, name-calling and even beating actual or suspected homosexuals are a real problem that schools must take seriously. But the inclusion of this form of harassment under Title IX drains the law almost completely of its original meaning. Which sex was it, exactly, that was being discriminated against when Jamie Nabozny's classmates called him a "faggot"? Nabozny wasn't subjected to hazing because he was a boy; he was picked on because he preferred the company of boys. Even the OCR was forced to admit that Title IX does not prohibit discrimination on the basis of sexual orientation, and congressional attempts to include this prohibition under the aegis of the law have so far been unsuccessful. Yet it is now the standing policy of the United States government to do just that: to treat the hurtful, though hardly sexually discriminatory, taunts of young children the same as it would a vindictive professor who flunks a student because she won't sleep with him.

THE "DOMAIN EXPANSION" OF sexual harassment under Title IX is just one aspect of the triumphalism of the law itself, but it is a significant one. The costs of the new liability of school districts for student-on-student harassment cases will be measured in millions of the taxpayers' dollars, spent not just on litigation but on new programs and curricula designed somehow to make naturally curious, rambunctious children fit into the narrow straightjacket of "sexually correct" behavior. A survey of elementary and high school principals after the *Davis* decision found that 60 percent expected an increase in sexual harassment litigation as a result of the ruling. And a full 65 percent said that programs offered by the school were being changed to respond to the increased liability. Basics of American education like gym class, shop, school dances and even recess are being cancelled. Fifteen percent of principals reported that spontaneous hugging was banned for fear of Title IX lawsuits.

Even discounting the costs involved, the expansion of Title IX sexual harassment raises serious questions about how we treat girls and women in schools today—and how we treat boys and men. In recent years American schools have become a tragic arena for a disheartening string of children, all of them young boys, who come to school and kill their teachers and classmates. In retrospect, some of these cases were preceded by warning signs: previous disciplinary problems, withdrawn behavior, a fascination with violent imagery. Some, even more dishearteningly, had no such signs at all. In the aftermath of these precocious homicides, we cast about frantically for answers. Why? Why would our young boys do such things?

For those who care about children—including many women's activists—finding the answer to this question should be a more worthwhile project than inventing new offenses for parents and their lawyers to use as political clubs against our schools and our kids.

FIVE

SEXUAL SELECTION

We shall be left behind with the blind, the lame, and the women.

> —Nathan Pusey, former president of
> Harvard, on the news that the draft
> would reduce the number of men
> applying to Harvard.

A T WHITEFISH BAY HIGH SCHOOL, just north of Milwaukee, seven of the eight National Merit Scholarship finalists last year were girls. That number is significantly changed from just three years ago, when only three of the eight finalists at Whitefish Bay were female. And the reason for the change isn't just the hard work of the girls there, although no one discounts their achievements. Bob Schaeffer, an anti-test activist 1200 miles away in Cambridge, Massachusetts, had something to do with it.

Schaeffer was one among a crusading band of opponents of standardized testing who set up shop in Cambridge in 1985 with a group called FairTest. On paper, FairTest is dedicated to the proposition that "tests should provide equal opportunity, rather than favor individuals on the basis of race, ethnicity, gender or income level." In fact, FairTest believes that standardized tests should be thrown out the window along with other educational tools that don't produce results that exactly mirror the race and gender balance of their subjects. The group has a long track record of battling alleged bias in the SAT and the other "high stakes" tests that are gaining favor in high schools and elementary schools.

Not long after opening its doors in the mid-Eighties, FairTest was contacted by a reporter from a small northeastern newspaper who had noticed what was, to her, a disturbing anomaly in the National Merit Scholarship competition. Six out of ten of the winners from the area were male, she told Schaeffer and his colleagues, but when she contacted local high school principals, they told her that the majority of their valedictorians and other academic standouts were female. What was going on?

What was going on, FairTest concluded, was gender bias in the selection of candidates for the prestigious prize. The sorting mechanism used to determine the semifinalists for National Merit Scholarships each year is the Preliminary Scholastic Assessment Test / National Merit Scholarship Qualifying Test (PSAT/NMSQT), more commonly known simply as the PSAT. More than two million college-bound high school juniors typically take the PSAT in any given year, and the top fifteen thousand scorers are automatically eligible for the scholarships. The "problem," according to FairTest, was that although around 55 percent of the test takers each year were female, young women received only about 40 percent of the top fifteen thousand scores. And of those who eventually received a National Merit Scholarship, only 40 percent were girls as well—despite the fact that the verbal section of the PSAT, where girls scored higher, is counted twice. This, to them, was evidence of bias in the test. "The PSAT wasn't measuring merit, it was measuring test-taking," says Schaeffer.

When he looked elsewhere, Schaeffer saw other scholarships based on standardized tests also denying girls their "fair share." New York State doled out its $250-a-year Regent's Scholarships and $2,000-a-year Empire Scholarships using SAT scores as its sole criterion. Since boys generally outscore girls on the SAT, girls were receiving fewer scholarships. So FairTest, along with Isabelle Katz Pinzler of the ACLU Women's Rights Project (who later went on to the Clinton Justice Department), took New York State to court under Title IX and won. A federal district judge found that the state's use of the SAT as the sole determinant of who received the scholarships discriminated against girls in violation of the federal law. The Educational Testing Service, which writes the SAT, consoled itself in the belief that the judge had not pronounced the test to be biased, but only ruled that New York State could not rely exclusively on it to determine scholarship winners.

Bob Schaeffer, however, saw the ruling as an opening to bigger and better things. The SAT itself, he thought, was now vulnerable to legal challenge for gender discrimination. Schaeffer also believed that FairTest's New York victory had set the stage for a challenge to the PSAT. So in 1994 he made a crucial decision. Instead of going to court against the National Merit Scholarship Program as they had against the state of New York, Schaeffer and his colleagues decided to go to Norma Cantu, head of the Department of Education's Office for Civil Rights. This decision, they understood, was a gamble; for once they filed a complaint of Title IX discrimination with the OCR, they would abdicate control over its outcome. But the politics of Title IX had changed in Washington since the late Eighties when FairTest had first taken on the Regent's and Empire scholarships. Cantu had signaled a willingness—even an eagerness—to promote FairTest's brand of socially engineered outcomes. Handing the case over to OCR, Schaeffer and his colleagues reasoned, was likely to produce just the result they were hoping for: the elimination of the test as a criterion for awarding the scholarships.

Before Cantu could go to work, however, there was one minor hurdle: the National Merit Scholarship Corporation received no federal money and therefore escaped OCR's jurisdiction. So FairTest, in conjunction with the American Civil Liberties Union, made the target of their complaint the Educational Testing Service and the College Board, the developers and administrators, respectively, of the PSAT. Both were private institutions but received federal funding in the form of contracts for testing services. On February 15, 1994, FairTest and the ACLU filed a civil rights complaint charging that the method of awarding National Merit Scholarships discriminated against girls under Title IX.

FairTest's complaint was supported, on the surface at least, by an undeniable fact: girls, on average, get better grades than boys. This is true among females of all ethnic groups, all ages and across all academic disciplines. Despite surpassing boys in the eyes of their teachers, however, girls score lower than boys on self-selected tests of academic achievement like the PSAT and the SAT, especially on the math sections. On the 1998 SAT, for instance, boys on average scored 35 points (out of 800) higher than girls in math and 7 points higher in English. On the PSAT, as well, the mean boys' score in math was almost three points higher than girls' (out of a possible 80) and .2 percent above girls' scores in verbal ability. So even with the verbal section (girls' stronger suit) counted twice in the final score, girls fared worse on the PSAT compared with boys. FairTest argued that these tests discriminate against females not only by failing to reflect their high school academic prowess, but also by failing to predict accurately how they will fare in college.

For its part, the College Board steadfastly denied there was bias in the test. Yes, it is true that boys tend to test better on the PSAT than girls, they conceded. It is also unquestionably true that more boys than girls tend to score in the 99th percentile of the PSAT, the qualifying threshold for the National Merit Scholarship. But the reason, they argued, isn't that the tests are biased toward boys. It is the way boys' and girls' test scores are distributed along the range of ability.

The College Board and ETS contended that what is known as the "spread" phenomenon was the culprit. In any test of intelligence or academic achievement, be it an IQ test or the PSAT, the scores of males tend to spread more to the extremes; that is, boys generally have more of the highest *and* lowest scores. If they are plotted on a graph, boys' scores form a bell curve with long flattening tails on both sides. Girls' scores, in contrast, tend to bunch up in the middle range of intelligence and ability. When they are plotted on a curve, the bell shape is tall, with relatively short tails on the two sides. This doesn't mean there aren't high-scoring (and low-scoring) girls and women; there are just fewer of them compared with men.

This "spread" effect isn't just particular to test scores. "On virtually every kind of variable—be it physical or mental capabilities or disabilities—you end up with more peculiarities among males," says Judith Kleinfeld, a professor of psychology at the University of Alaska at Fairbanks. "This had been noted since Darwin. It has been observed by people who study barnyard animals. Nature experiments with males, whereas women are a stable group."

According to Kleinfeld, tests like the PSAT and the SAT, which tend to attract higher-achieving students, magnify this effect. "Two things are happening here," she says. "First, you're going to get more boys among the top scorers because we're talking about those scores in the right-hand tail of the bell curve." (In two administrations of the SAT in the late 1980s, for instance, 19 out of every 20 perfect scores were obtained by boys.)[1] And something else is happening that lowers girls' average scores on the SAT as well. "More girls than boys—about 75,000 more girls—take the SAT," says Kleinfeld. "These are girls who are ambitious, and who want to go to selective schools and who work hard. But they are lower academic achievers and are less likely to have taken rigorous courses. The result is they pull down the average for girls."

As Kleinfeld and Christina Hoff Sommers have argued, the "spread" phenomenon works both ways. If it is "unfair" to girls that more boys score in the top percentiles on standardized tests, it is "unfair" to boys that so many of them score in the lowest percentiles. Boys are disproportionately represented among the lowest of the low achievers—in incidence of mental retardation, in learning disabilities and in special ed programs—as well as the brightest of the bright. But where are the lawsuits protecting them from alleged discrimination?

These arguments fell on deaf ears in Norma Cantu's Office for Civil Rights. Rather than be persuaded by the data, federal regulators were more sympathetic to the theories of female victimology advanced by FairTest. Asked by the *Dallas Morning News* to identify a particular question on the PSAT that was biased against girls, FairTest's Schaeffer was unable to do so. Instead, he averred, it was the multiple-choice format of the test that tipped the balance against females. "On average, girls tend to look for nuances and shades of gray," he said, in a statement that itself verged on sexism. "Boys are more inclined for quick answers."[2]

"The bottom line was counting bodies," said Gretchen Rigol, executive director of admissions and guidance services for the College Board, about the OCR investigation. And when all was said and done, OCR's body count showed, it believed, that the PSAT was guilty of discrimination against girls. Under threat of losing its government funding, the College Board reached a settlement with OCR in October 1996. Although they refused to concede that the PSAT was biased, the College Board and the ETS agreed to add a thirty-nine-question multiple choice test of written English—a test on which girls consistently score higher than boys—beginning with the high school class of 1999.

For FairTest, it was a qualified victory. Although it had not succeeded in eliminating the PSAT, it had established yet another precedent for mandated gender-based outcomes. Everyone understood that the addition of the written English test was designed to make sure that more girls qualified for the National Merit Scholarship. And FairTest lost no time in using the agreement to question the legitimacy of other standardized tests. "Why haven't similar changes been made in similar exams [which also show a 'gender gap' favoring men] such as the SAT and the GRE?" asked FairTest's executive director, Laura Barrett.

Why not indeed? If statistically representative outcomes are the definition of "fairness"—as the agreement between the College Board/ETS and OCR implicitly acknowledges—the changes made in the PSAT have produced a more just world for academically motivated high school girls. According to FairTest in 1999, the year in which the revised PSAT was first used to help determine National Merit Scholarship recipients, more than 45 percent of the awards went to girls—up from 40 percent when the OCR complaint was originally filed. What's more, FairTest says, the gap between boys' and girls' scores on the PSAT shrank by 40 percent the first year the new test was administered, and by another 26 percent in 2000. Still shell-shocked, no doubt, from its experience with federal "gender equity" enforcement, the College Board won't confirm or deny these numbers.

ALTHOUGH IT WAS A SIGNIFICANT breach in the tradition of merit-based academic measurement long claimed by the College Board and ETS, the successful campaign to bring about greater proportionality in scores on the PSAT was still an unfinished story for the OCR. The changes had occurred without the agency issuing a "policy" in the area of Title IX and testing. Educational institutions that had been so well schooled by OCR's mandate for gender quotas in athletics by the various Cantu-era "policy interpretations" were still lacking in official guidance on their responsibilities for "gender equity" in student assessment.

Adding urgency to the OCR's quest to remedy this situation as the 1990s advanced was a growing movement toward higher standards and merit-based criteria in education. In colleges and universities, affirmative action in admissions for women and minorities had suffered a series of setbacks in the courts (as in the *Hopwood* decision in Texas) and in the court of public opinion (as in California's statewide anti-preference initiative, Proposition 209). In high schools and grade schools, too, a movement toward higher standards, motivated by stagnant and declining student test scores, was gathering force. And as parents and taxpayers began to demand greater accountability for student learning and teacher performance, states began to institute standardized tests to measure the results of higher standards.

For liberal civil rights and education groups, the movement toward more merit-based criteria was a threat to the system of race and gender preferences in education that they had spent thirty years building and protecting. Yet arguing against higher standards in failing schools was not a politically viable option. So these groups turned their fire not on the standards themselves, but on the tests being instituted to enforce them. Like FairTest's case against the PSAT, the brief against "high stakes testing" (as the movement became known) is rooted in persistent race, ethnic and, to a lesser extent, gender gaps in test scores. Because educational advancement and opportunity are tied to performance on these tests, liberal civil rights and education groups argue they constitute illegal race and sex discrimination.

Norma Cantu made her hostility to high stakes tests known early. In 1994 the state of Ohio, as part of its efforts to raise academic standards, instituted a mandatory test of reading, writing, math and citizenship for all high school seniors who hoped to graduate. The results in the first year set off alarm bells in the anti-test community. Of the 2.6 percent of seniors who failed the exam, which was based on eighth-grade-level material, one-third were minorities. But after the state showed that students who failed the test had missed an average of 32 days of school their junior year, a federal judge ruled that the result had not been produced by bias. OCR stepped in to investigate anyway. It took a strong response from fourteen members of Congress—concerned that Cantu's effort to invalidate the Ohio test would damage the national standards movement—to get OCR to back off. And even then, it refused to concede that the investigation was an illegitimate exercise of federal power, or that racially disproportionate scores were not automatically indicative of discrimination.

It should have come as a surprise to no one, then, when OCR released its long-awaited codification of federal civil rights policy governing testing in 1999. Purporting to be only a "synthesis of settled law," the document in fact declared tests on which females and minorities fail to perform on par with males and whites illegal. "Nondiscrimination in High Stakes Testing: A Resource Guide" warned that the use of any test "which has a significant disparate impact on members of any particular race, national origin or sex is discriminatory and a violation of Title VI and/or Title IX, respectively." Schools would be able to use such tests only if they could show that the test is "educationally necessary and there is no practicable alternative form of assessment which meets the educational institution's needs and would have less of a disparate impact." The Education Department, which had spent three years producing the document, gave schools four days to provide feedback.

University administrators—many of whom routinely relaxed admissions standards, including test scores, to admit minority students—howled in protest. OCR had never complained when they overtly judged minorities by a different standard in affirmative action programs; so why were they now accusing them of doing so covertly with tests? The new OCR policy not only threatened that the use of standardized tests had to be justified as an "educational necessity," but mandated that cutoff scores under these tests had to be separately justified. But OCR failed to specify the point at which discrimination would occur. How many kids would have to be rejected for admission before a federal case could be brought? How many third-graders would fail to be promoted to fourth grade before they could get together and sue? This "major omission," commented former civil rights official Linda Chavez, was clearly "designed to intimidate educators" into abandoning the use of standardized tests altogether.[3]

The brazenness of the OCR testing document motivated even a generally complacent Congress to take action. Besieged by complaints from educational institutions, the House Education and Workforce Committee called Cantu to the Hill to justify herself. The OCR testing document, charged representatives on the Republican-dominated committee, fundamentally changed Title IX enforcement in schools by illegally importing a murky doctrine from employment law—know as "disparate impact" theory—into education civil rights enforcement.

Disparate impact theory is at odds with the common understanding of discrimination. Roger Clegg, an expert on anti-discrimination law, remarks:

> If you stopped the average man or woman on the street and asked them, "What is discrimination?" they would give you a definition that includes some element of deliberateness—that is, treating somebody differently because of a particular characteristic, whether it's race or sex or national origin. The disparate impact approach says that if, in the case of Title IX, you have some selection criterion that has a disproportionate effect on one sex or the other, then it's presumed to be discrimination. Proving that discrimination on the basis of sex was not the reason for the difference in outcome doesn't defeat the claim—it doesn't even have to be alleged that sex was the reason.

Students of Title IX detected strong similarities between OCR's "disparate impact" approach to standardized tests and its "proportionality" rule in sports. Athletics programs that offer women the same number of opportunities to participate in sports as men are nonetheless said to be discriminatory when women don't turn out in the same numbers as men. Likewise, the new testing standards don't accuse any of the people who design or administer tests of bias; they make their judgment, and prescribe their remedy, strictly on the basis of how the different races and genders score on the tests.

"When educators are told that the federal government is going to assume that any disproportionate effect is a violation of the law unless they can prove that there is some necessity for it, it puts enormous pressure on them to do one of two things," says Clegg. "Either avoid using the criterion and go to some other criterion that might not be as good, or make sure that the numbers come out right."

Although civil rights and education groups enlisted Clinton administration race advisor and Harvard University law professor Christopher Edley to quiet squeamish academics, the genie couldn't be stuffed back into the bottle. Under pressure from Congress, Norma Cantu backed off the draft regulations. While insisting that her first draft was simply a restatement of "settled law" and nothing more, she promised Congress she would remove the offending "disparate impact" language.

But, while avoiding the legal buzzword "disparate impact," the reissued OCR policy guidance—the federal policy that governs today—says essentially the same thing as the first iteration: "Tests are fair when they are valid and reliable for all students who take the tests," it reads. "The scores must not substantially and systematically underestimate or overestimate the knowledge or skills of members of a particular group." In other words, schools that use standardized tests do so at their own risk. As the *Chronicle of Higher Education* has reported, "The new guide continues to suggest test-use pitfalls in a way that may confuse colleges. Low scores can reflect that the test-takers don't know the subject matter well, the draft states. But if that lack of knowledge results from limited educational opportunities, then the use of scores to make decisions would be 'problematic.' "[4]

Pressure to do away with tests because of their disproportionate impact on one group or another comes from many sources, including some within colleges, universities, high schools and grade schools themselves. When the president of the University of California advocates doing away with the SAT he is seeking to please many different constituencies. But there is a difference—a critical one—between institutions deciding of their own accord to abandon standardized tests and the government forcing them to do so.

ADVOCATES OF DISPARATE IMPACT theory receive taxpayer-funded help in their crusade for gender-proportional outcomes through a law passed by Congress in 1974 called the Women's Educational Equity Act (WEEA).

In theory, WEEA was passed to fund enforcement of Title IX through the production of "educational" material dealing with sex discrimination in schools. But in reality, as Christina Hoff Sommers describes in *The War Against Boys*, WEEA is the U.S. government's contribution to a vast and expanding education "gender equity" bureaucracy. WEEA not only receives government funds to produce anti–sexual harassment guides for five-year-olds, it also makes grants to like-minded groups. The result is a logrolling circle of politically motivated academics and activists in which everyone is each other's grant-maker, grantee, best critic and publicist.

WEEA also sponsors "Edequity," an online forum for those who want to inject gender politics into the classroom. The chat on Edequity is just what is to be expected. Contributors opine about how our schools "shortchange" girls, how they dangerously "masculinize" boys, and how we need an "androgynous model of competence" to put a stop to the whole process. Much of the Edequity talk centers around a growth area of Title IX: how girls allegedly are discouraged from studying engineering, computer science and other subject areas that lead to lucrative careers. While introductory and intermediate high school math classes have about even numbers of boys and girls (or even majorities of the latter), girls lag behind boys in taking advanced math, physics and computer science classes. And although the gap is closing, women earn significantly fewer degrees in engineering, physical science and computer science in college and graduate school.[5]

The flip side of the overrepresentation of boys and men in math and science courses is their real and growing deficit in reading and writing ability vis-à-vis girls and women. So effectively has the case been made that boys' educational and emotional needs are being neglected, in fact, that some feminists are now working furiously to change the subject. The American Association of University Women, which almost single-handedly brought the gender wars into the classroom through a series of reports beginning with "How Schools Shortchange Girls" in 1992, is now busy trying to negotiate a ceasefire on the topic of girls' versus boys' academic achievement. The AAUW's latest report, "Beyond the Gender Wars: A Conversation about Girls, Boys and Education," focuses instead on the insidiousness of "gender ideologies" that keep both boys and girls "locked into roles" and determine the educational opportunities that will be available to them.

Still, there are plenty of activists who are unwilling to declare such a strategic truce in the gender wars. And because they can no longer claim that girls and women are being denied access to academic opportunities, they claim instead that they are being "steered" into disciplines with less earning potential. Yes, it's true that boys are being left behind in reading and writing, they admit, but what does it matter if they are destined to be the highly paid engineers and software programmers of tomorrow?

In an exchange dealing with the growing gender gap disfavoring boys, a frequent Edequity contributor named Linda Purrington, associated with an organization called "Title IX Advocates," displayed a chilling indifference to the plight of boys in American schools. "Does the reading/writing gender gap translate into fewer economic opportunities for men?" Purrington wrote. "If not, what is the concern?"

Imagine, for a moment, that someone had so blithely dismissed the right of young girls to be made functionally literate by the educational system the way Purrington dismisses the right of boys. The gender-feminist community would be hollering "hate crime!" But in order to capitalize on the erroneous public perception that a significant "wage gap" still exists between men and women with equal education and experience,* they dismiss the reading and writing underachievement of males as inconsequential. They are forced to concede that girls and women are excelling in most areas of education but insist that they continue to be "shortchanged" in the areas that count.

Or, alternately, they work feverishly to devalue girls' and women's gains. Commenting on the well-known fact that women now far outnumber men on college campuses, David Sadker, author of one of the sacred texts in the gender wars, *Failing at Fairness: How Our Schools Cheat Girls,* shows how the goalposts of "gender equity" shift as progress is made. "The female presence increases as the status of the college decreases," writes Sadker. "Female students are more likely to dominate two-year schools than the Ivy League. And wherever they are, they find themselves segregated and channeled into the least prestigious and least costly majors." In other words, all the gains of the last forty years that have made women the majority of undergraduates are an illusion. According to Sadker, higher female enrollment figures only serve to "mask the 'glass walls' that sepa-

---

*According to U.S. government National Longitudinal Survey of Youth data, among people ages 27–33 who have never had a child, women's earnings are close to 98 percent of men's. Occupation, seniority, absenteeism and intermittent workforce participation—in other words, choices made by women—account for pay disparities between men and women.

rate the sexes and channel females and males into very different careers." Teachers, professors, guidance counselors, parents and peers, so this theory goes, relentlessly herd girls into psychology, nursing, language and other courses leading to low earning potential, while men are free to dominate computer science, business, engineering and physics classes.[6]

For proof of this systematic bias against girls in course selection, feminists and federal regulators once again turn to numbers. The Office for Civil Rights' 1996 "strategic plan" identified "underrepresentation of women and minorities in advanced math and science courses" as one of the top priorities of the agency. And as is the case with sports, OCR targets schools for investigation based on statistical evidence that enrollment in these classes is not proportionate to student enrollment by race and gender. A "gender identifiable" classroom may have anything from a 10 to 20 percent disproportion of female students.[7] This is enough, according to OCR investigators, to initiate a probe and demand that the school show an "educational necessity" for whatever criteria it uses to admit students to advanced classes, be it course prerequisites or testing. And, as is also the case with sports, once OCR has them in its cross hairs for failing to show proportionality in a class, school districts typically accede to draconian "remedies" to improve female participation.[8]

The Clinton OCR bragged of having investigated almost forty school districts on the basis of underrepresentation of girls in math and science classes in 1997. But for activists both in and out of government, federal regulators weren't doing nearly enough to produce parity for girls and women as the information age dawned. So instead of focusing their efforts on improving math and science instruction for all students (American twelfth-graders had just scored near the bottom in math and science compared with twenty-one other countries and dead last in physics), they redoubled their efforts to draw attention to alleged barriers to scientific and technical achievement among girls and women. And in the waning months of the Clinton administration they received some help from an old and trusted ally, the U.S. Commission on Civil Rights.

ONCE DUBBED THE "CONSCIENCE of the nation" for its role in the civil rights struggle, the U.S. Commission on Civil Rights was, by the late 1990s, an agency in disarray. In 1997 the General Accounting Office released a devastating report asserting that the once revered civil rights watchdog was now plagued by mismanagement, questionable financial practices and shoddy staff work. Outside the scope of GAO's study but equally true was the fact that the Civil Rights Commission had also strayed far from its commitment to individual equality under the law. Its chairwoman, Mary Francis Berry, had famously said that "civil rights laws were not passed to give civil rights to all Americans," only to "disfavored groups" such as blacks, Hispanics and women. And the commission's work in the 1990s had come to reflect this group-rights ideology.

In 1997, the commission waded into the "civil rights" implications of using Title IX to increase elementary and high school girls' participation in advanced math and science programs. In a report entitled "Equal Educational Opportunity and Nondiscrimination for Girls in Advanced Mathematics, Science, and Technology Education: Federal Enforcement of Title IX," the commission called on the OCR to crack down on "significant barriers to math, science, and technology careers" for girls in American schools. Even for this controversial and highly politicized organization, the report was a sloppy piece of advocacy analysis. Some commissioners were appalled. Noting that it substantiated its conclusions with more than a hundred citations from a single source—the liberal activist American Association of University Women—a sharply divided commission refused to release the report.

But by 1999, when only two of the original four "no" votes remained on the commission, Berry was able to force the report through. Although it has largely escaped public notice, the USCCR document is an alarming compendium of the "inequities" perceived by gender feminists in schools today, and an echo of their belief that the federal government, under Title IX, should be brought in to correct them. All of the hallmarks of Title IX enforcement in sports—portraying girls and women as hapless victims, defining equity in terms of equal outcomes rather than equal opportunity, demanding that government play the mediating role between helpless women and a vast network of hostile male powers—are transferred to an analysis of access to math and science programs in the pages of the report. And, as ever, differences in achievement between boys and girls, however slight, are deemed to be the result of discrimination against girls.

While giving grudging credit to women's gains in education, the USCCR report strains to find areas in which they still lag behind men. Girls take more math classes than boys, it concedes, but then notes that they are less likely to enroll in physics classes and com-

puter science classes. They take more Advanced Placement tests overall than boys, it is true, but they are less likely to take AP tests in
calculus, science and computer science. These small deficits, the
report concludes, result from girls being "steered" away from these
subjects by gender-biased teachers, unthinking guidance counselors
and culturally backward parents.

But if the instances of "discrimination" the report points to are
slight, the consequences it infers from this alleged bias are sweeping. "Discrimination" against girls leads to fewer advanced degrees
in math, science and technology among women, and this, in turn,
determines the careers they choose. In one leap of logic, the report
attributes differences between men and women in the careers they
pursue, the jobs they choose and the wages they earn to systemic
bias in the nation's schools. "Differential interest and participation
in math, science, and technological endeavors ultimately results in
disparities in career options and lifetime earnings. Boys are encouraged to enter lucrative, growing fields such as engineering and
computer science. Girls are not encouraged equally. Such disparities could be diminished through stronger enforcement of Title
IX."[9]

The Civil Rights Commission heaps praise on the OCR's 1999
"policy guidance" outlawing standardized testing and urges it to do
the same for girls' access to math and science programs. The report
also encourages OCR to use the disparate impact theory to investigate schools in the absence of any allegation of discrimination. The
model it proposes—as if OCR needed to be reminded—is the
FairTest/ACLU campaign against the PSAT. A statistical "disproportion" in the number of girls in AP calculus, the report argues, is the
same thing as the statistically disproportionate number of girls who
used to qualify for the National Merit Scholarship. They are both
legally justified reasons for a federal Title IX investigation.

The commission's report also lends the weight of the government-
funded civil rights establishment to an increasingly popular bit of
Title IX mischief: the theory that sexual harassment, itself illegal
under the law, is the reason for the "underrepresentation" of girls
and women in advanced technical fields. Sexual harassment, the
report's authors assert, "can affect women's self-esteem and women's
participation in math and science courses." One of their "concerns"
is that OCR "hasn't made a link between participation in certain
areas like technology courses and sexual harassment." But beyond
repeating this point several times, the USCCR report itself fails to

establish this link—probably because it cannot be established. Do women in advanced mathematics and technical programs suffer higher levels of sexual harassment than women in other academic areas? The report offers no data. Is there evidence that physics classrooms and science labs are "hostile environments" for girls and women? The report fails to make its case even under this most liberal test of sexual harassment.

So questionable were the report's findings and so shoddy was the research cited to back them up that Commissioners Russell G. Redenbaugh and Carl A. Anderson took the rest of the Civil Rights Commission to task over the Title IX report. They repeated what male athletes and men's coaches had decried in Title IX enforcement for the previous eight years: by defining equity as "equal outcomes rather than equal opportunity," the Civil Rights Commission threatened to turn Title IX into a "quota machine." The dissident commissioners went on to say:

> In the absence of complaints or evidence of injury, there is no basis to assume, as this report does, that girls are unable to make their own choices or individual decisions and that they passively endure discrimination or "steering" out of fields that truly interest them. Moreover, if girls are being "shortchanged" or discriminated against, then why are they more likely to attend college and earn bachelors and masters degrees than boys? Why do girls consistently earn higher grades as high school students than boys in the face of such discrimination?

Most striking, Redenbaugh and Anderson pointed out, is the fact that "the greatest achievement gaps have to do with race, not sex"; and yet the commission concentrated only on differences in achievement by sex. Quoting sociologist Judith Kleinfeld, the dissent notes, "The shortchanged group is hardly female—it is African-American males." But instead of tackling this issue, the commission has chosen to focus on the "bogus crisis" of discrimination against girls in math and science.

Apart from a devastating critique of the U.S. Commission on Civil Rights' findings published in the *Washington Times* by behavioral scientist Patricia Hausman,[10] not a word of dissent from its accusations of bias against girls and women in math and science appeared in the media.

THE PUSH FOR GENDER-ENGINEERED outcomes in the technical fields of academia accelerated in 2000. A widely hyped settlement by the Massachusetts Institute of Technology with a group of female scientists endorsed a study (conducted by professor of biology Nancy Hopkins, the chief complainant of discrimination at MIT) that found a "universal problem" of discrimination against female faculty in terms of laboratory space, salary, research funds and other resources. The report was instantly—and uncritically—hailed as a milestone in equal rights for women. "Nancy Hopkins has done for sex discrimination what Anita Hill did for sexual harassment," reported the *Chronicle of Higher Education.*

Almost no one conducted a critical examination of Hopkins' work. But two who did—Judith Kleinfeld and Patricia Hausman, in separate studies for the Independent Women's Forum—found the report had methodological problems of a kind not normally tolerated at such an august educational institution as MIT. Kleinfeld and Hausman found that two-thirds of the committee that produced the report were female MIT faculty who stood to gain directly from its conclusions. (After submitting the report charging gender bias, all of the women were given pay raises and more resources. Hopkins herself received a 20 percent pay raise and saw her lab space and research budget tripled.)

But even more alarming to Kleinfeld and Hausman was the fact that MIT refused to release the data upon which the report's conclusions rested. "Where scientists disagree, the scientific community debates the evidence," says Kleinfeld. "But MIT will not release the data, making the absurd claim that such data as sex differences in laboratory space is 'confidential.' " Confronted with this criticism, the ladies of MIT backpedaled furiously. "This wasn't meant to be a study for the rest of the world," one of them said. "It was meant to be a study for us.... We weren't trying to prove anything to the world."[11]

Despite this expression of modesty, Hopkins and two other female MIT faculty responsible for the study brought together leaders of nine top research universities in February 2001 to sign a pledge to consider "potentially significant" changes in university policies to promote more "equitable" treatment of female faculty members. Officials from the California Institute of Technology, Harvard, Princeton, Stanford, UC Berkeley, the University of Michigan, the University of Pennsylvania and Yale all signed the pledge. And based on what evidence of "discrimination"? We may never know. MIT still refuses to release that data. But Patrician Hausman looked at available publication data for male and female biology professors at MIT and found one likely reason for the differences in salary and lab space that could be verified: the men worked harder than the women.

Hausman found that among more senior faculty, male biologists had markedly stronger publication records than females at similar stages in their careers. Three of six men had published more than a hundred papers in the past decade, whereas only one of five women had published as much. The rest of the aggrieved female biologists had published fewer than fifty papers each in the past ten years, less than all but one of the men.

David Gelernter of Yale watched his own university's desperate attempts to attract more female science faculty and concluded it can't be done. "Women are less drawn to science and engineering than men are," says Professor Gelernter.

> If you visit the comfortable, typical Connecticut suburb where I live, you can see the big picture in microcosm. The public schools run a summer program for children. Our older boy has spent a couple of weeks during each of the past several summers in a Lego-and-computers course. At the end of each session, students show off their accomplishments; I've never encountered one girl at any of these performances. Scientists and engineers are mainly grown-up versions of Lego-and-computers children. If you believe the Bigotry Theory, you must also believe that bigotry explains the scarcity of girls in our local Lego-and-computers group. If you believe *that*—that our tony, Democratic suburb is biased against little girls—then you'll believe anything.[12]

Gender activists, as obsessed with figures as numerologists are, have decided that we need more women in science anyway. And to move this project along, the federal government, through the National Science Foundation, sponsors an array of programs designed to entice little girls to be Lego-and-computers children. The NSF's "Program for Gender Equity in Science, Mathematics, Engineering, and Technology" doles out grants of $100,000 to $900,000 every year to promote more gender-proportionate math and science classes in kindergarten through college. The NSF also funds projects from Cambridge, Massachusetts, to Santa Barbara, California, to train teachers and produce curricula to promote "gender equity in math reform."

But what happens, asks Gelernter, when this project fails to attract more girls and women into the sciences? "The next step is frighteningly clear," he writes. Those "who are hot for affirmative action today will be hot for restricted admissions tomorrow." Think it could never happen? It already has. The "affirmative action pushers" who wanted women to play sports have been disappointed at the number of women willing to play, he writes, so they've begun to ax men's sports in the name of a "spurious equality." Says Gelernter, "If universities are willing to jettison aspiring male athletes in the name of equality, why not aspiring male physicists?"

IN THE LATE SIXTIES AND early Seventies, Bernice Sandler, "the mother of Title IX," laid the legal and public relations predicate for the passage of federal legislation outlawing discrimination on the basis of sex in education. Today, when she looks to the future of Title IX, she sees a growth industry in what she calls the "body issues." These issues—abortion, pregnancy, sexual assault and sexual harassment—"are still very much in development in terms of how we deal with them in the law," says Sandler. Title IX regulations already prohibit discrimination on the basis of "pregnancy, childbirth, false pregnancy, termination of pregnancy, or recovery therefrom" on the grounds that the foregoing conditions are a "temporary disability." Schools are already prohibited from expelling pregnant students, forcing them to take special classes or attend in separate facilities, or restricting them from extracurricular activities. But Sandler insists there is more room for growth.

One of the most notorious examples of this brand of Title IX enforcement comes to us from the Texas town of Hempstead, a 3,500-person hamlet about forty-five miles north of Houston. In 1993 the Texas chapter of NOW and the ACLU filed a complaint with OCR charging that Hempstead High School violated the civil rights of four of its sixteen cheerleaders when it kicked them off the squad for being pregnant. In the now familiar resolution of cases in which special-interest front groups threaten local school districts with the power and authority of the federal government under Title IX, the Hempstead school board saw what it faced, and settled. Complaining that the federal government was robbing communities of the ability to handle their own problems and set their own moral standards, the school board reluctantly reversed its policy of disallowing pregnant or parenting teens from holding elective office on campus. It also raised the required grade point average for cheerleaders from C to B. Because historically cheerleaders are girls, Texas NOW immediately complained that the higher standard was discrimination on the basis of sex. Threats of a federal lawsuit were once again raised, and once again the school district capitulated. Thanks to NOW, the *Dallas Morning News* opined, "high school cheerleaders in Texas won't have to worry about keeping up their morals or their grades."[13]

The Texas cheerleader case generated headlines, but a more recent Title IX case involving pregnant students has a potentially broader and more corrosive impact on standards in schools. In the spring of 1998, a board of teacher-judges of Kentucky's Grant County School District denied National Honor Society membership to high school juniors Somer Chipman Hurston and Chastity Glass. According to National Honor Society criteria, applicants are judged on four qualities: scholarship, service, leadership and character. At the time of their application, Hurston and Glass, both seventeen and unwed, had GPAs adequate for membership, but Hurston was several months pregnant and Glass had already given birth. The school district maintained that one of its criteria for judging character in applicants was abstinence from premarital sex. As Hurston and Glass had clearly engaged in such activity, Grant County officials didn't believe they made good role models for other students. Boys who could be established to have similarly engaged in premarital sex, they added, would also be excluded.

Expressing the hope of expanding Title IX protections of pregnant students, the ACLU jumped on the case and filed a lawsuit on behalf of the girls. "It's making a girl wear a scarlet P and bear the burden for something that is a joint activity," ACLU attorney Sara Mandelbaum told the *New York Times.* "No boy is being left out of the society for having engaged in premarital sex."[14] A federal judge agreed and ordered that Hurston and Glass be immediately granted NHS membership pending the outcome of their case. Then, in the familiar denouement of most Title IX cases, the Grant County School District settled, agreeing to pay both girls $999 in damages and promising not to violate Title IX in the future. For five years, the district will report to the ACLU the gender of applicants rejected from the society for sexual activity. For its part, the National Honor Society has been forced to notify schools that "non-selection of female students based solely on their condition of pregnancy or having given birth to a child in or out of wedlock" is forbidden as a violation of Title IX.

And in addition to protecting the "rights" of girls and young women to embark on the ill-advised path to teenage motherhood, Title IX activists are hard at work attempting to make the case that the federal law guarantees women the right to terminate their pregnancies as well. Earlier this year a group of female law students at New York University who call themselves Informed Students United for Reproductive Equity (INSURE) were shocked to discover that student insurance plans offered by the university did not include coverage for birth control pills and abortions. INSURE contacted the ACLU and together they approached the NYU administration, charging that their failure to provide birth control and abortion coverage discriminated against women in violation of Title IX. Not only were these "medically necessary" procedures not offered to women, they complained, but the school's failure to provide birth control led to more pregnancies, resulting in more abortions for which women alone must bear the financial burden. Not surprisingly, NYU gave in to their demands.

ANOTHER AREA IN WHICH Title IX is having a significant and ongoing impact in schools outside of extracurricular sports is in elementary and high school physical education classes. With the passage of the law, separate PE classes for boys and girls went the way of the dodo bird. And soon afterward, PE instructors began to notice something: in order to accommodate different levels of skill, strength and size, particularly among junior high and high school students, they were compelled to reduce gym activities to their lowest common denominator. Serious sports instruction gave way to fun and games. Football, soccer and gymnastics were replaced with aerobics, stretching and juggling.

What's more, embarrassed preadolescents had trouble competing shoulder to shoulder with one another. Boys laughed at less skilled girls, while hormones raged. "You've got some girls that are built like sexpots and the guys are all around her slurping at her," said a California PE instructor. "[Girls] feel embarrassed."[15]

Since the 1980s, phys ed requirements have been eliminated in many parts of the country. Today, only about 26 percent of high school students suit up for gym class every day. And the instruction that has survived, particularly among younger students, has been transformed by gender theorists who believe the elements of traditional sports—competition, an emphasis on physical strength, games that result in winners and losers—are patriarchal concepts in need of replacement with softer, more "inclusive" values. When they concern boys, at least, sports are regarded by women's activists as breeding grounds for criminals and wife beaters. Katherine Hanson, director of the Women's Educational Equity Act (WEEA) Publishing Center, believes sports promote a "culture of violence" among men and boys. "One of the most overlooked arenas of violence training within schools may be the environment that surrounds athletics and sports," she says.

The result is that in gym classes around the country, as the *New York Times* reported approvingly in July 2000, "the emphasis is increasingly on cooperation, not competition."[16] Dodge-ball is out (too "confrontational"), as is choosing up sides for teams ("egos are too easily wounded that way"). Instead, youngsters thrill to games of "non-threatening volleyball" and baseball games with no strikeouts; they frolic in gymnasium "no-fault zones" where "everyone is a winner," and write in "fitness journals" where they "express their feelings about various sports." In a "kinder, gentler" take on the traditional game of tag featured in these feminized gymnasiums, boys and girls "pretend they are fairies and skip around the gym with fluttering arms." Players who are tagged out can escape from captivity and rejoin the game by shouting "Free me!"

"The object is to accept everyone and their abilities," said Joanne Hamilton, a gym teacher in Sayville, New York. "As long as they do their best with their God-given talents and are kind, caring little people, they win."

Even the gym-class trauma previously known as the President's Physical Fitness Test has been transformed into a group-hug contest called the "President's Challenge." Where students used to try to pass a rigorous test of physical fitness and earn a coveted certificate (and rarely succeeded), today children perform a watered-down series of tests: some curl-ups, a one-mile run/walk, a shuttle run, some pull-ups and something called "the sit and reach." And nobody walks away without an award. "The idea now," said Christine Spain, director of research, planning and special projects for the President's Council on Physical Fitness, "is for everybody to be a winner."[17]

IN JUNE 1997, IN A ROSE GARDEN ceremony celebrating the twenty-fifth anniversary of Title IX, President Bill Clinton announced a dramatic new initiative. The law's reach should be extended beyond sports, Clinton told his audience of educators, athletes and women's groups. "Every school and every education program that receives federal assistance in the entire country must understand that complying with Title IX is not optional. It is the law and the law must be enforced," said the president. An administration official concurred, "We're not stepping up our enforcement of Title IX. We are *beginning* it."

They were ambitious words for an administration that had already, under the auspices of Norma Cantu and the Office for Civil Rights, ratcheted up spontaneous investigations of colleges and universities and backed Title IX quotas for female athletes in federal court. But in fact, for the vast expanse of government outside the Department of Education, the Clinton initiative did mark the beginning of Title IX enforcement. No longer would the Office for Civil Rights be alone in enforcing "gender equity" in federally funded education programs. Clinton directed the Department of Justice to begin drafting a government-wide rule, soon to become known by critics as the "Gender Quota Mega-Reg," so that each federal department, commission, regulatory body and independent agency would have Title IX enforcement authority.

Issued in its final form in the waning days of the Clinton administration, the potential of the "mega-reg" to extend gender quotas even further into American education is still untested. But surely the potential is there. Education spending by the federal government consists of $120 billion annually on more than 700 educational programs administered by some 39 separate federal entities. The Clinton rules not only expand the number of Title IX regulators by almost tenfold, they commensurately expand the ranks of the regulated. An analysis by leading education and legal experts put together by the Independent Women's Forum reveals that this new "reg" will "dramatically expand the scope of Title IX to cover even non-educational activities of federal, state and local agencies, as well as private institutions and businesses dealing with those agencies." Simply stated, this means that a business or a group no longer has to be a direct recipient of federal funds in order to be bound by the Title IX regulatory strings attached to those funds. Private firms that do business with educational institutions are now subject to Title IX regulation of all aspects of their business—even in activities not related to education, such as company-provided daycare or training programs.

Like the regulations that cover Title IX enforcement in athletics by the Department of Education, there is no language in the "mega-reg" that explicitly mandates sex quotas. Nonetheless, as we have seen, the relentless push for "proportionality" in athletics has already resulted in the most explicit federally enforced quota in American public life. This has occurred despite the absence of such a requirement in the regulations and, in fact, despite the explicit prohibition of an affirmative action mandate in the statute itself. The mega-reg, concluded the IWF analysis, gives other agencies similar latitude to change Title IX, "to follow the lead of the Department of Education in creating preference programs for women that use gender quotas as compliance measures." The myriad government-conducted training programs—from law enforcement training by the FBI to vocational rehabilitation services provided by the Social Security Administration—are now threatened with new scrutiny for evidence, not of sex discrimination, but of sex imbalance. Too many men in training at Quantico? Too few women getting daycare training from the Bureau of Indian Affairs? These are all now fodder for a federal sex discrimination case.

Perhaps most troubling is the likelihood that Title IX may affect government funding of medical and scientific research. The National Science Foundation gives over $109 million in assistance to undergraduate science, engineering and mathematics programs each year. Given that these programs are dominated by males, should that money be cut back to ensure that America graduates an equal number of female scientists, engineers and technologists? What would happen to the study of disease if the National Institutes of Health, which grant more than $200 million in funding to postsecondary schools, were ordered to allocate their budgets in a way that achieved "gender equity"? The Department of Health and Human Services, for that matter, doles out more than $70 million toward training nurses each year. Is it prepared to cut back on that training if fewer than half of those nurses are men?

Are these scenarios the stuff of fantasy? Asked recently if anyone in 1972 thought that men's sports programs would one day be eliminated because of Title IX, former Senator Birch Bayh, the law's original sponsor, said no: "That was not the purpose of Title IX. And that has been a very unfortunate aspect of this. The idea of Title IX was not to give fewer opportunities to men; it was to make more opportunities for women."[18]

A look back at the history of this law makes the future appear ominous.

SIX

WHY CAN'T A WOMAN
BE MORE LIKE A MAN?

Rep. Canady, reading from the Title IX statute:
*"Nothing [in the law] shall be interpreted to require any
educational institution to grant preferential or disparate
treatment to the members of one sex on account of an
imbalance which may exist with respect to the total
number or percentage of persons of that sex participating
in or receiving the benefits of any federally supported
program...."*
　　Rep. Waters, interrupting: *"Fifty-fifty! Fifty-fifty!"*
　　Rep. Canady: *"No, Title IX says no person in the
United States shall..."*
　　Rep. Waters, interrupting: *"It's the biggest quota
you've ever seen. It is fifty-fifty. It is a quota—[a] big,
round quota."*
—Hearing of the House Subcommittee
　　on the Constitution, June 1997

F EW DEFENDERS OF TITLE IX quotas are willing to announce their
position as openly as Congresswoman Maxine Waters. Most
advocates of gender-proportional outcomes, as we have seen,
prefer to cloak their support for quotas with high-minded appeals
to altruism and the need to rectify the wrongs of history.
Euphemisms such as "disparate impact" are frequently heard. But
the real agenda is never truly hidden: it is the creation of mandated
outcomes that pay no deference to human variety or the complex-
ity of individual desires and abilities. It is a social world governed
by one principle—as Representative Waters might put it, the principle of fifty-fifty.

　　The rationale for quotas under Title IX is that equal opportunity is
structurally impossible in a culture infected with power and privi-
lege. "Sameness of opportunity has not resulted in equity for
women," reads "Title IX: A Brief History" on the government-funded

Women's Educational Equity Act (WEEA) website. "Simply providing equal access does not challenge either the many deep-seated social beliefs about females and males and their respective abilities or the widespread practices that perpetuate these stereotypes." These congressionally sanctioned Title IX advocates go on: "Similarly, focusing only on equal treatment may serve to discount the existence of these prejudices by seeking to put the onus for change on the victims, thus serving to legitimize their oppression."

Evidence that women remain oppressed cannot be found in the real world, where they are ever more successful. So it is found in numbers. A world free of sex discrimination, in the view of Congresswoman Waters and WEEA, is a world in which participants in any given educational program perfectly match the number of males and females in the school itself. In this androgynous view of human nature, all girls and women and all boys and men are equally interested in and capable of playing lacrosse, excelling in physics, or scoring 1600 on the SAT. Any failure of this perfect equality of interests and abilities to manifest itself in equality of athletic and academic achievement, then, is prima facie proof of illegal discrimination under Title IX.

Any honest examination of a law must evaluate its central premise—in this case, that the sexes are identical in their interests and abilities. Congress can be forgiven for not conducting such an assessment in 1972 because Title IX, as it was originally passed, included no such presumption of sameness. Congress believed it was passing a law to guarantee equal opportunity. But today, as we have seen, Title IX is increasingly committed to equality of results. The question that is never confronted is whether this process is driven by a scientific understanding of how men and women would behave in a world without sex discrimination, or rather by politics.

Unfortunately, most of the debate on sex differences is only slightly more elevated than the exchange between Congressman Charles Canady and Congresswoman Waters that opens this chapter. Feminists don't even speak in terms of "sex" when discussing females and males; "gender" is now the default term. Why? Because unlike "sex," which connotes immutable differences between men and women, "gender" can be said to be "socially constructed." That is, the differences we observe between little boys and little girls are inculcated in them by social prejudices and power relationships. Girls are not by their nature more inclined toward Barbie dolls and tea parties than little boys are; they are taught by their perhaps unconsciously phallocentric parents and a culture saturated by male primacy that this is how they should behave. The same is true for little boys, who would be less prone to reenact WWF wrestling matches in their back yards if they weren't schooled by society in the violence and insensitivity of "masculinity." More recently, feminists and other progressive thinkers have advocated that gender roles be jettisoned altogether, arguing that designating people as "male" and "female" places arbitrary limitations on their freedom and creativity.

But for serious social scientists, as opposed to feminists and other political activists, the reasons for the differences between the sexes we observe every day are considerably more complex. Social scientists don't discount the role of environmental factors or socialization in producing girls who would rather play with dolls and boys who would rather play with guns; they simply discount these factors as *the* explanation of sex differences. Recent years have brought great advances in genetics, the understanding of male and female sex hormones, and evolutionary psychology. All of these have important things to say, not just about how men and women are different, but *why* they are different.

No one theory, it is true, fully explains why girls and boys and men and women behave the way they do, and in any case it is beyond the scope of this book to undertake a comprehensive review of the literature on the science of sex difference. What is pertinent to a discussion of Title IX is whether sex differences, as feminists claim, are "constructed" by the malign influence of a patriarchal society. If such differences are "socially constructed," we can deconstruct them through enlightened public policy. We can manipulate the different talents and passions of boys and girls to bring about the "fifty-fifty" world desired by Congresswoman Waters and all those for whom she speaks.

But if boys and girls are in some general way hardwired to pursue different interests and excel in different subjects, then it is time to take a serious look at a federal anti-discrimination law that has come to assume exactly the opposite.

EVOLUTIONARY PSYCHOLOGY, THE science of human behavior, draws from Charles Darwin in explaining the differences between the sexes. In humans' prehistoric past, this theory says, a natural division of labor accentuated inherent or "hardwired" differences between males and females. For millions of years, the males who were most likely to survive, attract females and pass their genes on to the next generation were those able to do what was expected of the stronger sex: vanquish their enemies in hand-to-hand combat, navigate long distances in search of food and fell game with weapons. Through successive generations, according to evolutionary psychology, males developed physical and behavioral traits associated with success in these activities, which in turn made them successful in the prehistoric dating game. The result is that today men are more aggressive than women and have a greater desire to seek dominance through competition. They are better at spatial reasoning and more adept at navigating than women. They throw objects farther and faster and hit their targets more often than women—not because their parents or the XFL encouraged them to do so, but because evolution made them that way.

This process, called "sexual selection," also produced distinctive traits in females. Their role as the bearer and caregiver of children made them, in general, more nurturing and risk-averse than men. Because they stayed closer to home and had to juggle multiple tasks—caring for children, gathering food, attending to other odds and ends around the cave—they developed better memory for the location of objects and landmarks. They sought dominance in relationships with other females, but generally did so with words rather than weapons, acquiring greater verbal dexterity than males.

Beginning at very young ages, little boys and little girls behave in ways that are entirely predictable to evolutionary psychologists. David Geary, professor of psychology at the University of Missouri at Columbia, has studied the play of young boys, still toddlers, at times when adults are absent and therefore unable to influence their behavior. Geary found that without prompting from adults, young boys are more physically active and engage in rough-and-tumble play three to six times more frequently than groups of girls at the same age.[1] According to Geary and others, the largest identified sex difference in physical ability among young children is in throwing distance and speed—the result of larger male forearms developed through millennia of throwing spears and clubbing enemies. As early as age two, 90 percent of boys can throw farther than same-age girls. By age four, 90 percent of boys can throw faster. By seventeen, only the most skilled girls can throw as far as the least skilled boys.[2] The boys are more likely than the girls to play in groups with established roles and hierarchies, and to do so in the absence of adult supervision. Over time, the play fighting of toddlers becomes the team sports of young boys and adolescents.

Geary refers to a 1994 study of 355 girls six to ten years of age and 333 same-age boys who were asked to record their play activities. The results:

- 44 percent of six-year-old boys regularly played football, compared with 2 percent of girls.
- 70 percent of ten-year-old boys played football, compared with 15 percent of girls.
- 85 percent of six-year-old boys and 86 percent of ten-year-old boys played basketball regularly, compared with 25 and 36 percent of six- and ten-year-old girls, respectively.[3]

As the above data indicate, team sports and rough-and-tumble play are not the exclusive province of boys; many girls engage in such activities often and eagerly. But in general, as evolutionary theory would predict, young girls are more interested in "play parenting" than in play fighting. In cultures as diverse as modern industrial America and the !Ko Bushmen of the central Kalahari, young girls are drawn to playing with dolls and acting out parental and family scenarios. Geary cites research finding that almost 99 percent of six-year-old girls and 92 percent of ten-year-old girls frequently played with dolls, compared with 17 percent and 12 percent of same-age boys (we don't know if this included "action figures" like G.I. Joe).

These findings confirm what most parents and teachers see every day, and what social scientists B. Sutton-Smith and B. G. Rosenberg observed thirty years earlier in studying play choices of preadolescents, findings that held constant "despite significant changes in the social roles of men and women in the United States," writes Geary.[4]

Feminist theory maintains, counterintuitively, that these differences between boys and girls are socially constructed—engineered by parents and other adults who reward "ladylike" conduct in girls and the contrary in boys. Thus children learn how to behave in accordance with stereotypes of the feminine and the masculine.

According to Stanford University psychology professor Eleanor Maccoby, however, it isn't society that teaches children to act like boys and girls. Looking at the behavior of children in groups of their peers, she concluded that they effectively teach each other to behave in sex-distinct ways. Maccoby has found that as boys and girls advance from toddlerhood to young childhood, they show a marked tendency to segregate by sex. At around age three, both sexes strongly prefer the company of the same sex. As childhood advances, this tendency increases, reaching its peak around the ages of eight to eleven. This phenomenon is reported across cultures, from advanced industrial societies to traditional preliterate societies.

Once separated into different playgroups, young boys and young girls begin to exhibit all the differences we discussed earlier. While both boys' and girls' groups engage in high amounts of physical activity, boys' play is markedly different from that of girls. Whether it's best friends seeing who can run the fastest or lift the heaviest rock, Maccoby writes, "Boys' games are more competitive than girls' games." Observation of the free-time play of fourth- and sixth-graders found that girls' games involved taking turns (one participant playing while others watch) 21 percent of the time, compared with just 1 percent of the time for boys. In contrast, boys engaged in direct competition with other boys—particularly between groups of boys—50 percent of the time, whereas girls did the same only 1 percent of the time. Maccoby postulates that what boys seem to be doing is establishing a dominance hierarchy. "The question of who is tougher than whom seems to be much more salient to boys than to girls, and more efforts to establish or maintain dominance may be seen among boys than among girls."[5]

What does this mean for groups of boys later in life? Among other things: sports. "In middle childhood, male competitiveness undergoes a structural change," writes Maccoby. "Boys in their larger groups tend to organize their competitive play in the form of structured games."[6] She notes that boys' interests "are expressed not only through participation in sports, but in a preference for watching sports programs on TV, trading baseball or football cards, talking about sports among themselves, and wearing caps or t-shirts that declare partisanship for certain teams."[7]

Maccoby is quick to add that sports are an absorbing activity for many girls as well. And although girls' groups show less interest in competition and athleticism than boys' groups, girls in general show broader and more varied tastes in activities than boys. What's more, individual girls have more freedom to cross sex lines and join in boys' play than a boy has to spend time in the girls' groups. This is because the rules are enforced more strictly among boys, who guard the purity of male identity more carefully than girls do their female identity. The adventurous girl who leaves her sisters to play with the boys is not sanctioned by her same-sex peers for crossing gender lines as much as a boy would be for crossing in the other direction.

Still, the blacktop jungle of childhood is mostly a sex-segregated place. And to the consternation of feminist social engineers and "gender equity" activists, this gender segregation defies attempts by adults to break it down. According to Maccoby, while adult coercion can produce temporary mixing of the sexes, children quickly revert to their separate camps when adult supervision is absent. She recounts an interview with an eleven-year-old girl who described teachers who try to make girls and boys play together more as "geeky ughs." One "geeky ugh" who made her class sit boy-girl-boy-girl in a circle and hold hands, the girl tells Maccoby, was particularly unpopular.[8]

Even when adults succeed in getting little boys and little girls to play together, the results often aren't what they desire. Christina Hoff Sommers tells the story of a feminist teacher in San Francisco who tried to break down the "glass walls" that separate preadolescent boys from preadolescent girls by getting the boys interested in quilting. The teacher asked the sixth- and seventh-grade boys in her class to make a quilt square dedicated to "women we admire." One little boy, Jimmy, chose the tennis player Monica Seles as the woman he most admired. And because Seles was attacked by a knife-wielding man, Jimmy stitched a bloody dagger on his square. "This must be an original in the history of quilting," says Sommers. "He thought it was cool. And his teacher thought he was a psychopath."

WHAT ABOUT SEX DIFFERENCES in other areas in which Title IX activists insist that the sexes, absent discrimination, would behave the same? Here the evidence points more clearly to distinctions in ability and interest. The existence of real and persistent male and female advantages in the "pattern of cognitive ability" and brain structure and function is not debated by most scientists.[9] Among the oldest truisms in social science is that females show advantage in verbal ability and males in mathematical ability.

The big question, of course, is why. Feminists are fond of laying these differences at the feet of teachers, guidance counselors, parents and test writers who, albeit often unconsciously, subtly "steer" girls away from math and science courses and toward preparation for less remunerative careers in the liberal arts. But as psychologist David Geary and Simon Fraser University psychology professor Doreen Kimura both point out, neither sex has an across-the-board advantage in these areas. In math, boys are better in mathematical problem solving and in translating complex word problems into diagrams,[10] but girls have the advantage in the calculation and computation parts of math aptitude tests.[11]

The fact that boys and girls excel in different areas of mathematics, taught by the same allegedly biased math teacher, shoots a hole in the theory of systematic sex discrimination as the source of differences in educational achievement, the theory favored by the U.S. Commission on Civil Rights. How are all these anti-female teachers cultivating female students who excel in computation, and get better math grades than boys to boot?

A likelier explanation for sex differences in math ability is the evolutionary division of labor between men and women. The male advantage in mathematical reasoning, many scientists argue, is the result of their greater spatial skills. The male's ancient role as hunter and warrior, according to Kimura, "would have put greater selection pressure on men to evolve long-range navigational skills, including, among other things, the capacity to recognize a scene from different angles or viewpoints."[12] The same kind of ability is used in "mental rotation" tests in which subjects are asked to imagine and describe what an object looks like from different angles. Men consistently outperform women on these tests, which could account for their advantage on the math portion of the SAT.

A similar explanation could account for women's advantage in some verbal tasks. Because conflict between women over the ages has been largely verbal, women were cultivating verbal dexterity while men were developing physical brawn. The need to "out-talk" their opponents has given girls and women an advantage over boys and men in the length and quality of their utterances, the speed and ease with which they articulate complex ideas and the speed with which they retrieve words from long-term memory.[13] There is evidence that this evolutionary linguistic advantage is transmitted through female hormones. Women, for instance, show greater verbal ability at certain times of the month. And female-to-male transsexuals lose their verbal fluency as they begin male hormone treatments.[14]

Could it be that the insights of Darwin, not a sexually "hostile environment," best account for the relative scarcity of female science professors at MIT? Doreen Kimura thinks so. Evolution has given women as a group "more person-oriented than object-oriented values," she writes. Men's advantage in spatial orientation has translated into more men than women studying and excelling in abstract, technical fields like physics and engineering. Even women who are equally gifted mathematically more often than not skip these fields in favor of less abstract disciplines that involve more contact with humans or animals. Of those mathematically gifted persons who pursue a career in biology, Kimura reports, over 23 percent are women, compared with less than 5 percent in physics and astronomy.[15]

Some "gender equity" enthusiasts point to a narrowing gender gap in math test scores as proof that sex differences can be erased through more enlightened pedagogy. "Gender differences in areas traditionally perceived as male such as spatial relations, have been eliminated by changing teaching practices, indicating that differences have more to do with socialization than with genes," reads WEEA's "Title IX: A Brief History." Doreen Kimura, however, is skeptical about such claims. The narrowing of the math-score gender gap, for instance, may be a function of changes in the tests rather than changes in skills. "If older samples [of test scores] contained more tests of 'mathematical reasoning' than more recent ones, an apparent change might appear over time which is actually an artifact of the particular kinds of tests being sampled," she writes.[16] What is needed is a comparison of the performance over time of similar groups of males and females on the same test items, a comparison made difficult by the rush to eliminate test questions that show large gender differences.[17]

THE MOST RECENT REBUTTAL of the theory of inherent sex sameness that underlies Title IX quotas comes in a vial marked "T." Testosterone, scientists are beginning to discover, is an important factor in the way physical and behavioral differences between men and women that have evolved over the eons are transmitted to us today.

Andrew Sullivan (a columnist for the *New Republic*) generated a record amount of reader mail to the *New York Times Magazine* in 2000 with his cover story detailing both his own experience and the research linking sex differences to testosterone. Sullivan, who began injecting himself with testosterone three years ago to compensate for low levels caused by HIV, believes passionately in equal opportunity for women. But he is also dismayed by the way advances for women have led to "the denial of biological and psychological differences between the sexes." Growing knowledge of the effects of "the big T" should refute once and for all this dangerous fiction, he concludes. Testosterone "helps explain perhaps better than any other single factor, why inequalities between men and women remain so frustratingly resilient in public and private life. The Big T correlates with energy, self-confidence, competitiveness, tenacity, strength and sexual drive."[18]

The *New York Times* called testosterone the "he hormone," but in fact, males and females both produce it. It's just that men have, on average, ten to twenty times as much as women. Psychologist and sex difference expert James McBride Dabbs, along with his wife, Mary Godwin Dabbs, reviewed the original research conducted on the testosterone levels of more than eight thousand men, women and children. Dabbs found that both between and within the sexes, the persons with the highest "T" levels are the aggressors, the risk-takers and the deviants. " 'Dominance,' " he writes, "is the theme that brings together the masculine qualities associated with testosterone."[19]

Dabbs asked thousands of men and women in different professions and different stages of the criminal justice system to give him saliva samples to test their T levels. What he found was in many ways predictable. Construction workers and NFL players have higher testosterone than the average guy. Trial lawyers have higher testosterone than tax attorneys. Combat veterans have more T than scientists, actors have more than ministers. Among both male and female prison inmates, violent criminals have more testosterone than nonviolent criminals. Delinquent youths are more saturated in testosterone than college students.

The amount of testosterone coursing through us at any given time varies according to environmental factors. Competition—or the anticipation of competition—increases testosterone in men (apparently, no research has been conducted to see if this same effect occurs in women). "Tennis players increase in testosterone when they win a tournament and drop when they lose," writes Dabbs. "They also increase in testosterone just before a match, as if in preparation." Even sports fans' T levels change with victory and defeat.[20]

What about the differences that testosterone creates between the sexes? It is not an exaggeration to say that testosterone makes *the* difference between males and females. Testosterone first appears in the second trimester of pregnancy, flooding the womb and turning the developing, sexually neutral fetus into a male. This *in utero* exposure to T influences later behavior. In fact, David Geary reports that preadolescent boys' overwhelming preference for rough-and-tumble play and group-level competitive play is "the clearest evidence for hormonal influences on human behavioral development."[21]

Girls can also be exposed to high levels of testosterone *in utero,* and when this happens it produces even more convincing evidence for the sex hormone's effect on behavior. This condition, called congenital adrenal hyperplasia (CAH), produces genetic females who act like boys. As youngsters, CAH girls exhibit "masculinized and defeminized play." They are more aggressive than non-CAH girls and they prefer trucks to dolls. And, interestingly enough, a study that compared CAH girls and unaffected girls found that almost 8 of every 10 CAH girls engaged in athletic competition more often than the average unaffected girl. This difference in propensity to play sports was almost as big as the gap between boys and unaffected girls. More than 9 out of 10 boys reported engaging in athletic competition more frequently than the average non-CAH girl.[22]

It is important to emphasize that all these social scientists warn that in the sex differences they have observed there is an overlap in the distribution of abilities in males and females. That is, within both sexes there is a range of ability and interest. Some girls are better than some boys in math and science, and some girls are more likely than their male classmates to turn out for the lacrosse team. The upshot is that none of the findings presented here can be used to make judgments about any individual man or woman. Yes, boys in general show a greater propensity toward team athletic competition than girls; but this doesn't mean we should conclude that any individual girl is less willing and able to compete than any individual boy.

Such an appreciation for the variety and subtlety of human nature is, however, not part of the worldview of those who enforce Title IX today. Instead of judging men and women by their individual interests and abilities, Title IX regulators direct their sweeping mandate on the sexes as groups. They prejudge the sexes to have identical interests and abilities. What's worse, they trample on the individual preferences of boys and girls and men and women by mandating outcomes so as to verify this prejudgment.

ONE OF THE MORE ENDURING questions of critics of Title IX is why, among all the extracurricular pursuits of American schoolchildren, enforcers of the law single out sports for gender quotas. Each year, for instance, bright young students come to Washington, D.C., to be finalists in the National Geography Bee. They are all academic standouts. They are all versed in the arcana of geography. (The winning question in the 2000 Geography Bee was, What are the three largest sections of Denmark? Answer: Jutland, Sjaelland and Fyn.) And with only two exceptions in the twelve-year history of the contest, they are all boys.

In a rare moment of clarity in the education gender wars, when the National Geographic Society formed a commission to look into the geography gender gap, it did not uncover a conspiracy against girls among geography teachers or gender-biased mapmakers. It found innate differences between boys and girls. "There are significant sex differences in levels of spatial skills in participation in geography-related activities like atlas use and navigation, and in the degree of liking geography," said the commission's co-chair, Penn State professor of psychology Lynn S. Liben. "I feel I have to say this as a woman. It's not true that every woman is worse than every man or every girl is worse than every boy. But at the group level, it is true. If you have to bet money, bet the man."[23]

What's most interesting from the perspective of Title IX is that these innate sex differences in geography have been nurtured not by teachers and other adults who might be accused of gender bias, but by boys themselves. Since most geography classes disappeared from American schools beginning in the 1950s, boys have had to study geography on their own time, in clubs and organizations after school. Girls, for their part, have shown less interest. When the teacher of the winner in the 2000 bee started an after-school geography club in Guilford, Connecticut, no girls showed up. "I always encourage the girls to get involved," Louis Russo told the Associated Press. "I don't want them to think it's an all-male situation. But they just don't pick up on it."

As it turns out, geography clubs are the rare male-dominated exception among after-school activities. Otherwise, girls overwhelmingly outnumber boys in participation in extracurricular activities. They outnumber boys in student government and honor societies, on school newspapers and in debating clubs. According to the National Federation of High Schools, 80 percent of choir members are girls and over 60 percent of debate club members are girls, as are members of high school orchestras. A strong majority—over 55 percent—of band members are girls.

Kimberly Schuld, a Title IX expert at the Independent Women's Forum, has calculated the losses girls would suffer if proportionality were demanded in after-school activities other than sports. Schuld found that if federal regulators followed the Maxine Waters Rule and demanded a 50/50 gender breakdown in debate clubs, almost 33 percent of current female debaters would be denied the opportunity to compete. Over 25 percent of female orchestra members and 36 percent of female choir members would lose out if "gender equity" were demanded in music. And perhaps most obviously, over 96 percent of female cheerleaders would be cut in a world in which Title IX was applied to extracurricular activities other than sports.

The National Federation of State High School Associations defines a sport as an activity that exists primarily for competition, is governed by the state, requires coaching and has a set season. Competitive cheerleading has all these things. It also demands physical fitness, athletic ability and discipline. The 64,000 girls who are on competitive cheerleading squads across the country compete against other schools; they have coaches and regular workouts that require intense preparation and ability in gymnastics, weightlifting and dance. Some states even regulate these squads as sports. But the U.S. Department of Education's Office for Civil Rights refuses to recognize competitive cheerleading as a sport to be counted toward the Title IX gender quota.

Why? It is a measure of the scorn Title IX activists have for what they regard as traditionally female pursuits—and the perverse reverence they have for traditionally male activities—that they refuse to recognize these talented and dedicated young women as athletes. Instead, they react to efforts to achieve Title IX recognition of competitive cheerleading as attempts by schools to "pad the numbers." Unless girls are behaving more like boys and less like girls, they don't meet the government's definition of what constitutes competitive athletics.

This closed-mindedness toward sex differences actually limits opportunities for girls and women, as can be illustrated by my own experience as a basketball player in grade school and high school in the late Seventies and early Eighties. My teammates and I played with a larger ball than girls play with today; it was designed to fit a man's larger hand. We didn't have a choice in the matter and our game suffered for it. We were less graceful ball-handlers and dribblers than the players of today, more prone to turnovers and missed passes.

Today, girls' and women's basketball is a much better game than my generation ever played. There are many reasons for this, including a broader pool of athletes from which to draw and more years of practice and experience for the average player. But one important reason is that the ball is smaller. The sport was changed to suit the smaller physical size of females, and this has made girls' and women's basketball not only more fun to play but more fun to watch.

Why not allow this same recognition of the differences between the sexes to change other sports—and bring new activities under the umbrella of athletics? Men's sports need not change but women should be allowed to put their own distinctive spin on sports. Instead of remaining relentlessly focused on defending the rare female placekicker on an otherwise all-male football team or going to Europe to recruit synchronized skaters, women's sports activists should look to activities like competitive cheerleading, dance and aerobics for which there is widespread and genuine female interest and ability.

On OPENING DAY 1994, Hillary Clinton threw out the first pitch for the Chicago Cubs while Bill Clinton did the honors for the Cleveland Indians. Bill let fly a credible toss, but Hillary muffed it. She was awkward, wrong-footed, pathetic. The contrast, portrayed in side-by-side photos in the next day's newspapers, was too much for feminist Colette Dowling to take.

"I could only imagine where things went from there," she wrote. "The First Lady wobbling forth her paltry pitch, an ill-concealed smirk spreading across the stadium as the men bonded in jocular superiority. Bottom line, they're thinking, Hillary isn't so tough after all. Bottom line, she throws like a girl."

Dowling is the author of a largely overlooked book that advances the provocative—and dubious—thesis that, given equal levels of athletic training, access and encouragement, women will achieve physical parity with men some day. "Studies show gender to be barely relevant as a predictor, or limiter, of athletic performance," she wrote in *The Frailty Myth: Women Approaching Physical Equality.* "What really counts are acquired skills, trained muscles, and movement efficiency that comes from refined technique." In other words, Hillary's problem on the mound in Chicago wasn't that she was genetically incapable of throwing as well as Bill, it was that she hadn't been given the chance to learn how. When young Bill was outside cheating at stickball, young Hillary was inside being forced to master the wifely arts of home and hearth. "The much ballyhooed skill of throwing a baseball is *learned*," Dowling asserted. "Boys aren't born with it."

Needless to say, most serious social scientists (at least those not mau-maued by political correctness) reject theories like Dowling's as animated by politics rather than by science. "The argument that sex differences are largely the result of socially imposed roles is appealing because such theories create an illusion of control," writes David Geary. "If the gender role theory were largely correct, then all sex differences in social status, social behavior, and so forth could potentially be eliminated by modifying the social expectations for women and men. While appealing, strong versions of this view are almost certainly wrong."[24]

How is it, then, that enforcement of one of our most powerful and comprehensive federal laws is based on this flawed view of human nature? Part of the reason is expediency.

"There's no question in my mind that women are less interested in playing sports than men," said Lamar Daniel, a former OCR investigator, to *Reason*'s Michael Lynch. "But logically, in my experience, you can't prove that. It's just not provable."[25] Judges and government officials charged with determining what's "fair" in sports programs that are segregated by sex are sorely tempted by—and too often succumb to—numerical solutions. It's neater, it's cleaner and it's easier just to slap a formula on Title IX compliance, label it "statistical proportionality," and get home in time for supper. In the Brown University case, the appeals court called Amy Cohen's argument that Brown was discriminating against women because it hadn't yet reached proportionality "far more serviceable" than the defense's contention that fewer women were interested in sports than men. All the talk of different interests and abilities, sniffed the judges, "brings up thorny issues of proof."

Yet proof does not appear to be a criterion applied to the other side. Our public policy governing sex discrimination in schools rests on a view of men and women that no one but the most radicalized gender feminists believe. And it is based on a radicalized double standard. Feminists are eager to assert the equality of women in every arena of competition with men, yet they are unwilling to cede the political power that attaches to the mantle of victimhood. So they try to have it both ways—and have thus far been overwhelmingly successful. Disregarding the illogic, they assert the equality of interests and abilities of men and women while at the same time demanding special protection for females.

"What's so distorted about this is that the universities, by having single-sex teams, have *already* created additional opportunities for women," says Maureen Mahoney, author of Brown University's appeal to the Supreme Court. "If they said we're just going to have coed teams and we're going to select based on ability, women would be aced out in most sports solely on the basis of objective performance ability. So what they've done is that they've created opportunities for women where they couldn't achieve them simply on the merits by having single-sex teams, and now they're told that by doing that, they must make it fifty-fifty."

Of course it's ludicrous to insist that women and men compete for spots on the same sports teams—but that's the point. The law sensibly recognizes this and makes allowance for sex segregation in athletics. But women's activists have used this segregation to carve out preferences for women that extend far beyond the playing field. Their delicate balancing act—insisting on special treatment for women at the same time as they insist on the sameness of the sexes—reflects the increasingly tenuous position of feminism in American public life today.

For the older generation of feminists, like Colette Dowling, the enduring belief seems to be that women will never achieve equality with men until they become just like men; until the Hillary of the future hums a fastball on opening day with the same velocity as the future Bill. For them, even to talk about difference is to imply inequality. It's understandable that women, whether they call themselves feminists or not, would seek to end discrimination. But why, one wonders, should we want to become just like men in the process? Social science teaches us that there are real and persistent differences between the sexes, although no individual boy or girl or man or women is defined by these differences. Sadly, those who enforce Title IX today assume precisely the opposite: that there are no inherent differences between the sexes, and that every individual man and woman can be defined by this androgyny.

On the other hand, a younger generation of women, who have come of age after the tumult of the Sixties, is more comfortable with differences between the sexes, and less intent on abolishing them. For these women, it's possible to be a capable athlete without becoming like a boy. It's okay to be a girl.

One summer night, having recently purchased a very spiffy miniature football at the Baltimore ESPN Zone, I was tossing it back and forth outside with a friend of a friend. As I let loose an uncharacteristically wobbly throw, a stranger passing by remarked, "You throw like a girl!" His young daughter, walking with him, angrily retorted, "She *is* a girl!"

Colette Dowling and her hardcore feminist sisters could learn a thing or two from her.

SEVEN

LEVELING THE PLAYING FIELD

Title IX is not about percentages and numbers. Title IX is about halting practices of discrimination. It's not a quota bill.

—Norma Cantu

T HE ELECTION OF GEORGE W. BUSH in November 2000 has led to speculation by friends and foes alike of Title IX quotas that the "gains" of the 1990s might be reversed in the new millennium. Thanks to a group of wrestlers and ex-wrestlers called Iowans Against Quotas, who ingeniously used the popularity of their sport in Iowa to approach presidential candidates in 1999 and 2000 before the all-important Iowa caucuses to solicit their views on Title IX quotas, George W. Bush was on the record on Title IX before he was his party's nominee.* His statement was supportive, but qualified—perhaps as definitive as could be hoped for from a candidate whose party is plagued by a persistent gender gap at the polls.

"I support Title IX," read the Bush statement. "Title IX has opened up opportunities for young women in both academics and sports, and I think that's terrific. I do not support a system of quotas or strict

---

*Presidential aspirant and former New York Knick Bill Bradley was approached on the campaign trail in Iowa in 1999 by a member of Iowans Against Quotas, ninth-grade wrestler Clarke Davidson. When Davidson asked Bradley at a campaign stop in Des Moines if he supported proportionality, Bradley played dumb. "What's proportionality?" he shot back. But Bradley knows very well what proportionality is. In 1993 he served as a consultant to an NCAA Gender Equity Task Force charged with developing guidelines for schools struggling to comply with Title IX. In its final report, the task force declared that the "ultimate goal" of NCAA member institutions should be that "the numbers of male and female athletes are substantially proportionate to their numbers in the institution's undergraduate student population."

proportionality that pits one group against another. We should support a reasonable approach to Title IX that seeks to expand opportunities for women rather than destroy existing men's teams."

On paper, the prospects for reform of Title IX appear to be excellent. Contrary to the law's more excitable defenders, ending quotas would not entail repealing Title IX or even amending it. The proportionality test is not law; it's not even regulation subject to congressional approval. It is simply a bureaucratic decree, a policy interpretation issued pursuant to a regulation that was issued pursuant to a statute. If the Bush administration's Office for Civil Rights wants to change the Title IX athletics policy to exclude the proportionality test—or change any other Cantu-era policy interpretations, reinterpretations, guidance or what-have-you—they can simply issue new policy.

But then again, it's not that simple. Before the new Bush administration even had the chance to appoint a secretary of education, the Women's Sports Foundation fired a Title IX warning shot across its bow. "Under the provisions of the federal Administrative Procedures Act, if the Office for Civil Rights...wishes to change the regulations or current policy interpretations, OCR would be required to issue a 'Notice of Proposed Rule Making,' " the WSF reminded its supporters in the spring of 2001. "OCR would then be required to designate a reasonable period of time for public comment, usually 30 to 60 days, before it could issue changes in regulations." The WSF, then, "would have the option of submitting comments. The Foundation would not favor any change that weakens this law and results in unequal treatment of female athletes."

A veiled threat? To be sure. And the Women's Sports Foundation is just the vanguard of an army of seasoned veterans of the gender wars who stand ready and eager to defend the territory they've gained under Title IX. To make sure that a risk-averse Republican president doesn't make the mistake of thinking he can take on the Title IX lobby with impunity, these gender warriors point to the results of a 2000 NBC News/*Wall Street Journal* poll that seems to show widespread public support for Title IX quotas:

> Q: *Title Nine is a federal law that prohibits high schools and colleges*
> *that receive federal funds from discriminating on the basis of gender.*
> *Title Nine is most commonly invoked to ensure equal opportunities*
> *for girls and women in high school and college athletics. Do you*
> *approve or disapprove of Title Nine as it is described here?*

Yes, approve of Title IX: 79%
No, do not approve of Title IX: 14%
Do not know enough about it: 4%
Not sure: 3%

> Q: *To comply with Title Nine, many schools and universities have had to cut back on resources for men's athletic programs and invest more in women's athletic programs to make the programs more equal. Do you approve or disapprove of cutting back on men's athletics to ensure equivalent athletic opportunities for women?*

Yes, approve of cuts: 76%
No, do not approve of cuts: 19%
Not sure: 5%

It is interesting, to say the least, that feminists now take refuge in a poll showing widespread public support for cuts to men's programs that they insist are not occurring as a result of Title IX. Still, is there credence to their claim that the American public supports elimination of men's opportunities under the law? Only if we assume that the NBC/*Wall Street Journal* poll is an accurate portrayal of how the law is enforced today. The survey asked the public if it would support cutting back on resources for men's athletic programs and investing more in women's to make the programs "more equal." Who but the most hardhearted misogynist wouldn't support those two words?

But as we've seen, at issue under Title IX isn't the fair and equal division of resources between men and women, but an attempt by the federal government to dictate how men and women should behave. Female athletes have more teams to choose from in colleges and universities today than male athletes. They receive more athletic scholarship aid per capita than male athletes. The battle for "gender equity" is not a battle for resources; if it were, women's groups would have declared victory some time ago. The struggle is about power and ideals.

In their attempt to prove that all differences between the sexes are socially created, feminists have been willing to sacrifice the interests of males for the manufactured illusion of an androgynous ideal. Imagine, for a moment, what the public's reaction would be to a survey question that accurately portrayed the way the law is enforced:

> Q: *To comply with Title IX, many schools and universities have had to eliminate men's opportunities to participate in sports—including unfunded opportunities—in order to ensure that no more men than*

*women are athletes on college campuses. Do you support eliminat-
ing men's opportunities to create a 50/50 gender balance in school
sports programs while positions on women's teams go unfilled?*

This is not how the pollsters who conducted the survey for NBC
News and the *Wall Street Journal* asked the question because it is
likely that this is not how they understand the law to be implemented. Journalists—even ink-stained veterans—routinely describe
compliance with Title IX in terms of the equal sharing of resources
between men and women in athletics. The result is that it is rare for
a citizen who picks up a newspaper or turns on the television to see
coverage of the law that is not glowingly positive. And it is a rare
politician or government official who will tell the truth about the
law's enforcement today. The first step toward re-leveling the playing
field between the sexes in our schools, then, is simply beginning to
tell the truth about Title IX.

IN THE SPRING OF 2001 an ad sponsored by the Independent Women's
Forum appeared in the *Daily Bruin*, UCLA's student newspaper, purporting to expose "the ten most common feminist myths." Myth
number nine, "gender is a social construction," was answered thus:

> While environment and socialization do play a significant role in
> human life, a growing body of research in neuroscience,
> endocrinology, and psychology over the past 40 years suggests
> there is a biological basis for many sex differences in aptitudes and
> preferences. Of course, this doesn't mean that women should be
> prevented from pursuing their goals in any field they choose; what
> it does suggest is that we should not expect parity in all fields.

The impact of this ad on the UCLA campus was immediate and
explosive. Rallies were organized. The women's center demanded
that the *Daily Bruin* "retract" the ad, apologize for it and promise
never to commit such apostasy again. When the newspaper's editor
defended the running of the ad as an exercise in free speech, Christie
Scott, head of the campus feminist "Clothesline Project," dismissed
this rationale as "somewhat cowardly."

"Somewhat cowardly" is the wrong term to apply to the editors of
the *Daily Bruin,* but the right term for most participants in the discussion of women's role in American life today. Few topics involve
more disinformation and shaving of the truth on the one side and
political cowardice on the other. Christina Hoff Sommers (the author
of the UCLA ad), Judith Kleinfeld, author and psychiatrist Sally Satel
and others have done an excellent job of uncovering the disinfor-

mation and false statistics used by women's advocates to advance their agenda. But they are virtually alone in this thankless task. For far too long, a wittingly or unwittingly gullible media has treated even the most outrageous claims of feminists as fact. The effect has been to give artificial life support to the myth that girls and women are an oppressed minority, clinging weakly to their rights only with the assistance of the full weight and authority of government.

This effect is magnified where the arcana of Title IX enforcement are involved. Under President Clinton, pro-quota bureaucrats followed their administration's well-practiced strategy of deny, deny, deny when confronted with accusations that the law was resulting in losses for men. Consider this statement by Norma Cantu, which appeared in *Insight* magazine in 1998: "Nothing in Title IX or OCR's enforcement policy requires or encourages schools to cut men's sports. A school can choose to drop a men's team in order to provide substantially proportionate athletic opportunities for men and women students. But, neither Title IX nor OCR require or encourage this as a way to reach that goal."

This, from the civil rights enforcer who in 1996 declared proportionality the "safe harbor" for schools struggling to stay on the right side of the federal law. This, from a high-ranking official in an administration that supported the creation of a "remedial purpose" for Title IX in *Cohen v. Brown.* This, from the civil rights activist who declared that tests on which different racial groups and sexes fail to score equally are a violation of federal law.

The federal government, in fact, has enforced a quota standard in Title IX athletics for much of the past decade. This enforcement has been opportunistic; not every school has fallen under OCR scrutiny and been forced to cut men's teams, add women's teams or do both to achieve proportionality. And this fact is yet another layer of deception in OCR's insistence that the federal government does not force Title IX compliance through a gender quota. Schools don't need to experience a federal investigation or a lawsuit to know that there is no "safe harbor" short of proportionality, and that their athletic departments are not under their control unless and until they reflect the gender breakdown of their student bodies. They've read the "policy interpretations"; they've seen how OCR has treated schools like the University of Wisconsin and Boston University; and they've seen how the courts have ruled on the Brown and Cal State Bakersfield cases. American education has received the message loud and clear.

Why isn't there more acknowledgment of the reality of Title IX enforcement among education officials and in the education press? Quota critics point to an atmosphere of extreme intolerance to dissent from Title IX orthodoxy on campus. Time and again, coaches I spoke with refused to allow their names to be used for fear of losing their jobs. Even coaches who had already lost their jobs in Title IX cuts refused to go on the record for fear of not finding new jobs on other campuses. It is a measure of the power of liberal women's rights activists in academia today that universities are unable—or unwilling—to complain as the federal government micromanages more and more of their affairs in the name of "gender equity." When so-called "women's issues" are on the line, defenders of institutional autonomy like Brown's Vartan Gregorian are distressingly rare. When Gregorian stood up against excessive federal intrusion on his university in the Cohen case, none of his fellow Ivy Leaguers stood with him. Perhaps that's only because he didn't succeed in his challenge. "These people are extremely sensitive to social criticism," says Brown counsel Beverly Ledbetter about the claustral world of academia. "They will hide behind whatever good result happens—they won't open their mouths to get any good result, but they will hide behind any good result."

Even among students whose lives are most affected by Title IX quotas, there is little questioning of the need or the rationale for federally mandated gender equity. Students have an admirable commitment to fairness and opportunity for women, but they are numbed by the bureaucracy that enforces the current definition of equity. "Nobody questions the underlying assumptions of Title IX, that male and female students will be equally interested in organized sports and that a lack of proportional numbers must indicate something is 'wrong,' " says Robert Geary, professor of English at James Madison University. "Universities are supposed to be places of inquiry, but some subjects appear closed to scrutiny—too sensitive. Students seem caught in a vise of bureaucratic rules which are combating ills that may well not exist at all."

Title IX quotas have never been the subject of debate. They were created outside the electoral process by unelected government officials working hand in hand with special interest groups. The first step toward ending gender quotas, then, is to demand the truth from those who insist they don't exist.

• *Demand that government officials acknowledge that they "encourage"*

Title IX compliance through quotas: In June 1999 the Northeast regional office of the OCR sent a letter to the athletic director and administrators of Central Connecticut State University warning that they must add twenty female athletes to their sports roster to comply with the federal law. CCSU had already brought the percentage of its athletes who are female from 29 to 49 by dropping men's wrestling and adding women's lacrosse. But females made up 51 percent of the students at CCSU, so OCR insisted that twenty more female athletes were needed. In the fall of 2000, the University of Wisconsin at Madison received a similar letter. Having labored for a decade to attract women to programs, UWM had achieved near-perfect parity in the spring of that year: 429 athletes on campus were men and 425 were women. Not good enough, said Algis Tamosiunas, director of OCR compliance in Chicago. Because females now consti-tuted a majority of students on the Madison campus (53.1 percent), the school would have to add another 25 women.

Letters like these are routinely sent from the OCR to schools struggling to stay on the right side of the federal authorities. OCR officials such as Norma Cantu are being dishonest when they insist that because the regulations don't "require" sex quo-tas, those who administer the regulations don't work relentlessly to make quotas happen. Proportionality is the threshold test for Title IX compliance in federal regulation. It is the standard con-sistently supported by the Clinton administration in the courts, the standard adopted by the courts and the only guarantee that a school will not be exposed to a federal investigation or a law-suit. It is *the* standard for compliance with Title IX today. To say otherwise is to lie, plain and simple.

• *Demand that "neutral" organizations like the NCAA represent all athletes, not just the lucrative and the politically correct:* In the deeply cynical belief that Title IX quotas will never threaten big-time football and men's basketball programs, the NCAA has left men's nonrevenue sports like wrestling and swimming to fend for themselves against Title IX quota cuts. It has not only looked the other way when men's programs are eliminated to meet Title IX gender quotas, it has acted to encourage these cuts.

Since the early 1990s, the NCAA has required that the "ulti-mate goal" of NCAA member institutions be that "the numbers of male and female athletes are substantially proportionate to their numbers in the institution's undergraduate student population." The NCAA's five-year-plan certification process is a reiteration of the OCR's three-part test, with an unmistakable emphasis on proportionality. In addition, its biennial "Gender Equity Study" of member institutions provides a benchmark against which the NCAA measures progress toward fulfillment of the sex quota. Commenting on the data in the 1999 report, NCAA president Cedric Dempsey ignored cuts to men's programs and instead lamented insufficient statistical progress on the women's side: "As we move closer to proportionality, we recognize improvements will not be as dramatic. We've made some progress, but must continue to press for compliance."

Cheryl Levick, chairwoman of the NCAA Committee on Women's Athletics, echoed his thought: "The rate of growth in participation numbers and dollars spent is much too slow. In the new millennium, every university, conference and the NCAA must have a primary goal of equalizing these numbers."[1]

Like the OCR, the NCAA takes refuge in the defense that it doesn't "require" cuts to men's programs to achieve gender equity. But the NCAA, again like the OCR, doesn't need to "require" cuts officially in order to be complicit in losses to men's programs. As long as revenue-making men's sports like football and basketball are immune from cuts geared toward gender equity (and for the time being at least it appears they are) the NCAA has been content to allow all of the pressure that Title IX quotas place on athletic programs to be absorbed by men's nonrevenue sports. But if it purports to represent all intercollegiate athletics—and to place limits on their scholarships, recruiting and play—the NCAA has a moral obligation to speak up for men's teams that are being hurt by its craven acquiescence in gender quotas.

- *Call a preference a preference:* Honorable people can disagree over whether or not government should institute preferences to help previously disadvantaged groups—yet Title IX quota advocates refuse to allow this debate. Perhaps they understand that where there has been open debate on the utility and fairness of preferences, such as in California with Proposition 209 in 1996, citizens have generally chosen to keep government out of the business of counting by race and gender.

Deborah Brake of the National Women's Law Center is

typical of those who refuse to call a preference a preference. "A lot of the opponents of Title IX like to talk about proportionality and to say that the test of compliance is only one of proportionality," she said. "And the reason they do that I think is a cynical one. They try to tap into some of the anti-quota and anti-affirmative action sentiment that's out there and try to talk about Title IX as if it were a quota."[2]

If the proposition were put to them directly, many Americans might well agree that affirmative action for girls and women is justified and appropriate. But this has not occurred with preferences under Title IX. For political reasons, straight talk has been avoided and those who describe Title IX as a quota regime have been vilified as attempting to erase the hard-won gains of girls and women.

There is no honor in subverting the democratic process so as to force a policy on the public that government officials don't have the courage to call by its proper name. It's time to let some sun shine on the topic of sex quotas in education, and let the people decide.

EVEN THOUGH THE PUBLIC DOES not yet have an accurate understanding of how Title IX is being implemented today, there are storm clouds on the horizon for use of this law in schemes involving gender equity.

The period of Title IX quota expansion during the past decade has also been a time of relative prosperity for colleges and universities. In some cases, this has meant that schools struggling to meet the gender quota in athletics could do so in relatively painless ways, by adding women's sports and/or limiting men's participation by cutting walk-ons. As long as the funds were there, providing the scholarships and building or upgrading facilities for new women's teams was relatively easy.

A slowing economy combined with escalating expenses in athletic programs, however, threatens to change this. Financial reports filed by schools under the federal Equity in Athletics Disclosure Act show that athletic department budgets in NCAA Division I schools in 1999–2000 were up more than $1 million from two years earlier, reaching an average of $11.2 million. For the schools that field the most competitive football teams, budgets were up more than $2 million, to an average of $28.7 million.

Growing budget pressures come from a variety of directions, of course. One significant financial pressure point is the cost of expanded women's programs. Budgets for women's sports are rising faster than those for men's sports, as is spending on scholarships for women. Another financial strain is accommodating the growing desire among athletic directors and fans alike that teams be competitive on the national level. Less and less are sports treated as another part of a well-rounded educational experience; increasingly, teams must justify their existence by winning. This compulsion is helping to fuel an "arms race" in spending, not just on big-time football and basketball programs, but on women's teams and men's nonrevenue sports as well. According to the *Chronicle of Higher Education,* nonrevenue teams in NCAA Division I cost roughly $220,000 on average in 1999–2000. And at big-time football schools, where more money is available to fuel the spending arms race, women's teams and men's nonrevenue squads cost up to half a million dollars apiece.[3]

These exploding costs have already triggered a fresh round of budget cuts. And because women's sports can't be touched, the sacrifice is borne by men's teams. Iowa State University, the University of Kansas and the University of Nebraska have all recently begun major cuts to their men's athletic programs. The bad news for Title IX quota advocates is that these rising budget pressures give schools a new incentive to go to court to argue that women's programs should be fair game for budget cuts as well.

A school that invites a lawsuit by cutting a women's team or failing to create a new team to meet the gender quota might very well decide to fight back in court rather than be forced to incur costs it can't afford. Alternately, male athletes whose positions are eliminated might decide to take a cue from Duane Naquin, the Boston College senior who was denied entry to Mary Daly's class on the basis of his sex and who sued to win his right to coeducation. As that case showed, if there is one thing university administrators fear more than accusations of gender insensitivity, it's lawsuits. In the Mary Daly case and others to come, public interest law firms like the Center for Individual Rights have been effective in reversing the course of sex discrimination in our schools.

Although Title IX preferences have yet to be struck down in a federal district court (and thus made a prime target for Supreme Court review), creative legal challenges in the right circuits could yield results for fairness and gender-blind policies. "I have no doubt that the Supreme Court will take the case if and when there is a split in the circuit courts," says Maureen Mahoney, who argued Brown University's case to the Supreme Court. "And I also have no doubt that there will be a split in the circuit if schools litigate this issue in circuits where it's undecided." Women's advocates have been careful so far to push for Title IX quotas in liberal district courts that are likely to agree with their version of equity. But according to Mahoney and others, bringing the right challenge to Title IX quotas in the more conservative Fourth Circuit which covers Maryland, South Carolina, North Carolina, Virginia and West Virginia, or the Fifth Circuit, including Texas, Louisiana and Mississippi, could bring a judgment that restores the original intent of the law.

The rising cost of fielding intercollegiate athletic teams is also contributing to a reexamination of how sports fit within the mission of the university. All recruited athletes, male or female, receive a preference from college admissions committees. But preferences for female athletes—and arguments for female quotas within athletic programs—are often justified on grounds above and beyond the contribution these women make to sports teams. Make women athletes, we are told, and you make better women. With some justification, women's groups argue that girls who play sports are associated with such positive traits as higher graduation rates, less drug use, higher self-esteem and lower levels of teenage pregnancy.

In a much-anticipated book, *The Game of Life: College Sports and Educational Values,* James Shulman of the Andrew W. Mellon Foundation and former Princeton University president William Bowen examine what kind of students are currently being admitted to schools under athletic preferences. Using the same database that provided the intellectual fodder for Bowen's earlier defense of race-based affirmative action in education—data on 90,000 students who attended 30 selective colleges and universities in the 1950s, 1970s and 1990s—the authors claim that of all the recipients of affirmative action in colleges and universities today, female athletes are the most preferred. At a "representative" nonscholarship school in 1999, Shulman and Bowen found, a female who is a member of a minority had a 20 percent admissions advantage, the daughter of an alumnus had a 24 percent advantage, a male athlete had a 48 percent advantage and a female athlete had a 53 percent advantage. That is, *a female athlete had a 53 percent better chance of being admitted than a nonathlete with the same SAT score.*[4]

And what are schools gaining from this admissions preference? *The Game of Life* sets out purposefully to shoot down the various "myths" of intercollegiate athletics, chief among them, in Shulman and Bowen's view, that athletics builds character. Shulman and Bowen argue that athletes today are less academically prepared, less concerned with scholarship and more financially directed than their fellow students. But what is most interesting about their analysis is their finding that these traits are increasing among female athletes as well as male.

Whereas female athletes were once at least as academically qualified as other female students, Shulman and Bowen found that they now lag behind other female students. Even using twelve-year-old data, which reflect trends that certainly have only deepened with the increased scope and competitiveness of women's sports, the authors saw a distinct pattern of decline, particularly among athletes in the highest-profile women's sport: basketball. They looked at the SAT scores of female athletes and women in the student population at large between 1976 and 1989 and found a gap disfavoring female athletes that widened appreciably in the thirteen-year period. Among female basketball players, athletes had SAT scores 177 points lower than other students at public universities and 240 points lower at private schools.[5]

Female athletes are also developing a grade-point-average gap with female students—following, with a lag, that between male athletes and other male students—a gap that cannot be explained by socioeconomic status, SAT scores or field of study. Whereas in 1976 female athletes were less likely than other female students to rank in the bottom third of their class on graduation day, by 1989, 39 percent of female athletes finished in the bottom third of their class as opposed to 29 percent of other female students. This poorer showing by female athletes, moreover, was especially pronounced among athletes who were heavily recruited. In NCAA Division I-A private schools, almost half of female athletes—49 percent—landed in the bottom third of their class, compared with 29 percent of other women. (At NCAA Division III schools, which don't offer athletic scholarships, female athletes fared much better.)[6]

Another benefit frequently cited to justify preferences for female athletes under Title IX is the racial and ethnic diversity they bring. But Shulman and Bowen found that, "contrary to some popular impressions, more aggressive recruitment of women athletes is not bringing disproportionately large numbers of African American women to campuses (as it is in the case of the male athletes in the high profile sports)." In NCAA Division I-A, the number of minority women on campus has increased as a result of more female athletes on campus. But "in every other set of schools, the share of African American women playing intercollegiate sports is much lower—even half the corresponding percentage of African American women in the student-at-large category." What's more, these numbers declined between 1976 and 1989,[7] more evidence that Title IX has produced gains for white girls, not minorities.

The trend in women's athletics, particularly in the most competitive, high-profile sports, is away from the ideal often claimed by Title IX quota ideologues. Instead of representing the female ideal at the start of the twenty-first century—tough, smart, confident and empowered—female athletes are beginning to resemble the dimwitted, half-civilized male athletes of the feminist stereotype. And in such a situation, the rationale that women's preferences under Title IX are justified because they create better students and better citizens becomes hard to sustain.

ANOTHER CLOUD DARKENING THE future of gender quotas under Title IX is the failure so far of women's sports to attract the fan base and revenue potential that many men's sports enjoy.

The success of Women's World Cup soccer awakened in many women's groups a deep yearning to take women's athletics to the next level by making it financially viable. The Women's Sports Foundation recently declared a "Brave New World" for girls and women in sports in which they don't just get a place on the playing field, they get big bucks for playing. "Initially the primary function was opening doors of opportunity," said Donna Lopiano at the WSF's fourteenth annual conference in 2000. "Now, it's exploiting the participation of women in sports in the economic sense, gaining access to assets, program expansion and addressing the continuing problem of girls being discouraged from sports."[8]

The evidence from women's professional athletics, however, is that the Women's Sports Foundation faces a daunting challenge. Today, five years after the launch of the Women's National Basketball Association (WNBA) and less than a year after the debut of the Women's United Soccer Association, gender equity may still be more politically profitable than financially rewarding. The WNBA has yet to turn a profit, and average attendance at games is down from its peak three years ago, as are television ratings.

It turns out that the social engineers are even more wrong in their contention that men and women are equally interested in watching sports than they are in their assertion that men and women are equally interested in playing sports. Many girls and women are dedicated and enthusiastic participants in sports, but when it comes to being a fan—buying a ticket for a game or watching one on TV—men are still the economic force driving the sporting industry. According to Lawrence Wenner of Loyola Marymount University in Los Angeles, about 20 percent of men but only 4 to 5 percent of women can be described as "strong, committed" sports fans. Men outnumber women among viewers of major sports telecasts by 2 to 1. They even watch women's sports more than women do.[9]

This gender gap in sportsmania shows up in support for coverage of women's sports in the print media as well. Whereas *Sports Illustrated* goes out each week to about 3.5 million subscribers, *Sports Illustrated for Women* comes out only once every two months, with a circulation of 400,000. Conde Nast gave up on *Women's Sports and Fitness* in 2000 after spending two years and a reported $45 million trying to find an audience.

Lopiano and others rationalize the small crowds at women's sporting events with the argument that the women's sports market needs time to mature, that the female sports fan is an "emerging" fan. In many respects this is true, but the for-profit world of women's professional athletics is very different from the subsidized world in which the "gender equity" battle has so far been fought. Financial investors, unlike college administrators, can't be coerced into providing the resources necessary for women's leagues to survive. According to Stefan Fatsis, sportswriter for the *Wall Street Journal,* several owners of NBA franchises—who also own the local WNBA teams—would rather not have to continue the women's teams, but they have been ordered by NBA commissioner David Stern to "stick with it." Over half of the women's teams are even turning to marketing directly to lesbians through events like "gay pride night" to expand their fan bases in some cities. This kind of marketing, however, carries a risk of alienating some fans. Last year, the WNBA put out a list of married and engaged players, a move seemingly designed to appeal to its fan base of families with children.[10]

As I WRITE THIS, THE University of Kansas has eliminated its men's swimming and tennis teams, citing financial pressures and federal gender equity requirements. Bucknell University has announced it will drop wrestling and men's crew as varsity sports, eliminating forty-four men's positions in order to reach statistical proportionality in its athletics program. Seton Hall, Capital University in Columbus, Ohio, and the University of St. Thomas have all dropped their wrestling teams. Iowa State has eliminated baseball and men's swimming. The University of Nebraska has also axed men's swimming and diving, leaving only four of the schools in the Big 12 conference still participating in the sport. The Big 12 is now questioning whether it will continue to stage a men's swimming and diving championship or do away with it altogether, a move that will almost certainly result in the remaining schools eliminating their men's programs.

This denial of opportunity for men is occurring because a group of people with a narrow agenda has worked hard and successfully behind the scenes to make it happen. Driven by the desire to overcome real discrimination against girls and women that was once widespread, activists like Bernice Sandler, Donna Lopiano and Norma Cantu and groups like the Women's Sports Foundation, the National Women's Law Center and the American Association of University Women set out to create preferences for girls and women. They sought out and co-opted friendly government officials. They initiated a shrewd legal strategy when friendly government officials were unavailable. Partly through government fiat, partly through a shared ideology, they built a phalanx of promoters and defenders of "gender equity" on college campuses and in high schools and grade schools across the country. They wooed their allies and cowed their enemies in Congress and insisted that both parrot their message. They conducted a highly effective and sophisticated media campaign. They helped draft regulations and interpretations of regulations and interpretations of interpretations of regulations. At each stage in the legal and bureaucratic evolution of Title IX, they out-thought, out-worked and out-cared the people whose opportunities were being destroyed. The edifice of discrimination these activists built is a testament to their commitment.

Now there is a movement aborning to challenge the arrogance of that power. Individuals bringing lawsuits challenging discrimination against boys and men under Title IX may or may not bring relief, but a new candor in our discussion of Title IX can help create the political predicate for reform.

In the end, of course, it is up to those charged with enforcing our laws to apply Title IX honestly and forthrightly. This is not, needless to say, a politically painless proposition. After some significant rollback of race-based preferences in the 1990s, elected officials and even conservative activists seem to have lost their appetite for battling identity politics. To stand on principle, many seem to believe, is to risk appearing "mean-spirited" in an age when compassion is the opiate of the electorate.

Writing about the "conundrum of quotas" in the *Wall Street Journal* in the opening months of the Bush administration, Shelby Steele noted that conservatives have a hard time not appearing mean when they stand on principle on the issue of race because they lack moral authority. "Were conservatives of the last generation fastidious about principles when segregation prevailed as a breach of every known democratic principle, including merit?" wrote Steele. "Can conservatives now, when it so conspicuously suits their convenience, look the former victims of racism in the eyes and say, 'Now we're ready to enforce a discipline of principles for everyone'?"

The equation of race preferences with sex preferences under Title IX is not perfect. As we have seen, there are real, innate differences between the sexes of the kind that cannot be shown to exist between people of different races. Even so, Steele's point can easily be applied to conservatives on the issue of sex today. Conservatives of the last generation certainly did not lead the charge for women's rights—properly understood to be the same rights before the law that men historically have enjoyed. It was liberals, of course, who took the battle for women's rights forward. Eventually they corrupted it into a separatist movement in which women's interests are portrayed to be at odds with those of men. Nonetheless, before feminism took that destructive turn, conservatives did not champion the cause of equality for women, and more often than not they resisted it.

Can we now credibly argue that the principle of gender-blindness be upheld in the laws meant to guarantee it? Liberalism has been suborned on the issue of sex quotas. Can a conservative administration challenge quotas for girls and women without appearing "mean" and losing the thin margin of centrist voters who put it in office—voters who would most likely oppose gender preferences if they knew they existed but who nonetheless distrust conservatives on issues involving women? This is a hard political equation, a "conundrum" of sex quotas every bit as difficult as Shelby Steele's conundrum of race quotas.

The way out of this conundrum is the same as it was in the 1920s when women struggled for the right to vote, and the same as it was in the 1950s when blacks encountered segregationists at the schoolhouse door. The way out is to defend the principle of nondiscrimination, even when it is hard. *Especially* when it is hard.

And liberal feminist groups will make it hard to stand on this principle; they will challenge the moral authority of those who seek to restore the original intent of the law. But the principle of nondiscrimination that is embodied in the original intent of Title IX has stood the test of time. It has allowed girls and women to rise from uncomfortable interlopers to become the dominant force in American education. Conservatives can gain new moral authority by insisting on standing by this principle and resisting a distortion of the law that discriminates against a new group of victims and demeans the very achievements of the girls and women it purports to protect.

Re-leveling the playing field in American education will not be easy. But those who go into this battle have at their side two often underrated assets: First, it's the law. And second, it's the right thing to do.

ACKNOWLEDGMENTS

I have a number of individuals and institutions to thank for their support of this book. My gratitude goes to the Bradley Foundation and to Bill Kristol and Gary Schmitt of the New Citizenship Project for their indispensable financial and moral support. I thank Peter Collier and Encounter Books for seeing potential in this issue, and in me, in supporting this book project.

I thank the many athletes, parents, coaches, professors and administrators both named and unnamed who shared their stories with me. Leo Kocher, head wrestling coach and associate professor at the University of Chicago, in particular, deserves the gratitude of all men and women—both athletes and non-athletes—who are committed to fairness and genuine equity. When and if sanity is restored to educational athletics, the nation will have Leo to thank.

My thanks go to the group of courageous, independent women who inspired this book and have inspired millions of other young women to question feminist orthodoxy. Christina Hoff Sommers, Judith Kleinfeld, Danielle Crittenden, Maureen Mahoney and Jennifer Braceras all contributed, both directly and indirectly, to the ideas and arguments advanced in these pages. It is no accident that most of these women have, at one time or another, been associated with the Independent Women's Forum (IWF), which has done more than any other women's organization to seek truth and advance justice for women. I particularly want to thank Barbara Ledeen, under whose energetic leadership the IWF became a force to be reckoned with, not to mention the nation's greatest advocate for returning Title IX to its original anti-discrimination mandate.

Finally, to Jonah and Cosmo: thanks for being there for me. I will always return the favor.

Jessica Gavora
Washington, D.C.
December, 2001

NOTES

Introduction

1 David Margolick, "Women Turn to Courts to Gain Rights," *New York Times,* 29 June 1982.
2 Ibid.
3 Abby Goodnough, "Rights Group Says Sex Bias in New York Vocational Schools Denies Women High Tech Skills," *New York Times,* 18 August 2001.

Chapter 1

1 Stephen Buckley, "Second-Class Soccer Citizen," *Washington Post,* 16 July 2000.
2 The connection between the two events was too close for comfort. President Bill Clinton and his wife, Hillary, had agreed to be honorary chairpersons of the Women's World Cup just days before the president was forced to go on national television and acknowledge an "inappropriate relationship" with former White House intern Monica Lewinsky. The announcement of his involvement in World Cup soccer was delayed until February 1999, after his impeachment and subsequent acquittal in the Senate.
3 Christine Brennan, "The Year of the Hero," *USA Today,* 2 December 1999.
4 Ann Gerhart, "Cashing In on the World Cups," *Washington Post,* 14 July 1999.
5 Cary Goldberg, "Facing Forced Retirement, Iconoclastic Professor Keeps on Fighting," *New York Times,* 15 August 1999.
6 Peter Monaghan, "Dropping Men's Teams to Comply with Title IX," *Chronicle of Higher Education,* 4 December 1998.
7 Rebecca Trounson, "Victory at a Cost," *Los Angeles Times,* 30 January 2001.
8 The American Association of University Women Legal Advocacy Fund, "A License for Bias: Sex Discrimination, Schools and Title IX," 2000, p. 3.
9 General Accounting Office, "Gender Equity: Men's and Women's Participation in Higher Education," Report to the Ranking Minority Member, Subcommittee on Criminal Justice, Drug Policy and

Human Resources, Committee on Government Reform, House of Representatives, December 2000, p. 4.

10 Terry Eastland, *Ending Affirmative Action* (New York: Basic Books, 1996), pp. 48–49.

11 The California State University, *Report under the CSU/Cal-NOW Consent Decree Regarding Equal Opportunity in Athletics for Women Students*, February 2000, tables 5–7.

12 "Office for Civil Rights Puts Bite on Sex Bias in Athletics," *Women in Higher Education,* June 1994.

13 *New York Times,* 10 November 1993.

14 Charles Murray, *What It Means to Be a Libertarian* (New York: Broadway Books, 1997), p. 53.

15 National Federation of State High School Associations, Annual Survey of Athletics Participation.

16 General Accounting Office, "Gender Equity: Men's and Women's Participation in Higher Education," p. 17.

17 Ibid., p. 15.

18 Molly Cummins, "Many Coaches Argue Law Helping Women's Sports Hurts Men," Knight Ridder, 21 September 2000.

Chapter 2

1 Jonathan Feigen, "Texas Lawsuit May Change Face of College Athletics across U.S.," *Houston Chronicle,* 27 June 1993.

2 *New York Times,* 10 May 1995.

3 Paul Daugherty, "Call Me a Swine: Title IX Is Wrong," *Cincinnati Enquirer,* 16 April 1999.

4 Jonathan Feigen, "Gender Equity: Football Coaches Circle the Wagons," *Houston Chronicle,* 28 June 1993.

5 *Congressional Record,* 15 July 1975, pp. 22777–778.

6 Welch Suggs, "Gap Grows between the Haves and Have-nots in College Sports," *Chronicle of Higher Education,* 17 November 2000.

7 Gilbert M. Gaul and Frank Fitzpatrick, "Rise of the Athletic Empires," *Philadelphia Inquirer,* 10 September 2000.

8 R. Bruce Billings and Donald Aythe, "The Role of Football Profits in Meeting Title IX Gender Equity Regulations and Policy," *Journal of Sport Management,* vol. 14, no. 1 (January 2000).

9 Welch Suggs, "Uneven Progress for Women's Sports," *Chronicle of Higher Education,* 7 April 2000.

10 Welch Suggs, "At Smaller Colleges, Women Get Bigger Share of Sports Funds," *Chronicle of Higher Education,* 14 April 2000.

11 Gilbert M. Gaul and Frank Fitzpatrick, "Women's Sports: The Ink Is Mostly Red," *Philadelphia Inquirer,* 10 September 2000.

12 *USA Today,* special series on the 25th Anniversary of Title IX, 13–20 June 1997.

13   Barbara Carton, "You Don't Need Oars in the Water to Go Out for Crew," *Wall Street Journal,* 14 May 1999.
14   *San Diego Union Tribune,* 2 April 2000.
15   The California State University, *Report under the CSU/Cal-NOW Consent Decree Regarding Equal Opportunity in Athletics for Women Students,* February 2000, p. 16.
16   *National Desk,* PBS, April 1999.

Chapter 3

1   Erik Brady, "Brown Gymnasts Still Fighting to Compete," *USA Today,* 8 June 1992.
2   Allison Lobron and Lockhart Steele, "Tennis Coach Recalls 'Strange' Offer," *Brown Daily Herald,* 4 December 1994.
3   Debra E. Blum, "A Victory for Woman Athletes," *Chronicle of Higher Education,* 28 April 1993.
4   Lynette Labinger, "Finding the Meaning of Fair," *New York Times,* 17 September 1995.
5   Joshua Weisbrod, "University Awaits Title IX Appeal," *Brown Daily Herald,* 5 September 1995.
6   Joshua Albertson and Lockhart Steele, "Trial Kicks Off with Pettine's Caustic Questioning of Brown," *Brown Daily Herald,* 27 September 1994.
7   Alison Lobron and Lockhart Steele, "Lies, Damned Lies and Statistics?" *Brown Daily Herald,* 14 November 1994.
8   Joshua Weisbrod, "Conclusion of Trial in Sight," *Brown Daily Herald,* 27 February 1995.
9   Joshua Albertson and Lockhart Steele, "Title IX Court Case Begins," *Brown Daily Herald,* 27 September 1994.
10   David Roach, *Washington Post,* 5 October 1995.
11   U.S. Department of Education Office for Civil Rights, 1990 Investigator's Manual, p. 25.
12   *New York Times,* 9 May 1995.
13   Lisa Guernsey, "Many Female Athletes at Brown U. Are Ambivalent about Ruling," *Chronicle of Higher Education,* 6 December 1996.
14   Welch Suggs, "U. of Washington Makes Waves by Dropping a Women's Team," *Chronicle of Higher Education,* 18 August 2000.
15   *Chronicle of Higher Education,* 6 October 2000.

Chapter 4

1   Scott Heller and Alison Schneider, "Boston College Feminist Fights Order to Allow Men in Her Class," *Chronicle of Higher Education,* 5 March 1999.
2   *New York Times,* 15 August 1999.
3   Tamar Levin, "Students Use Law on Discrimination in Sex-Abuse Suits," *New York Times,* 26 June 1995.

4   American Association of University Women Legal Advocacy Fund, "A License for Bias: Sex Discrimination, Schools, and Title IX," Washington, D.C., 2000.

5   Catharine A. MacKinnon, "Sexual Harassment: Its First Decade in Court," *Feminism Unmodified: Discourses on Life and Law* (Cambridge: Harvard University Press, 1987), p. 107.

6   Anita K. Blair, Richard P. Ward, Peter L. Ebb and Jennifer C. Braceras, Brief of Amicus Curiae, Independent Women's Forum, December 1998.

7   Daphne Patai, *Heterophobia* (Oxford: Roman & Littlefield, 1998), p. 13.

8   Ron Southwick, "Professor's Swearing Created Hostile Environment in Classroom, Appeals Court Rules," *Chronicle of Higher Education,* 5 March 2001.

9   Ben Gose, "Brandeis Lawsuit Puts Campus Courts in the Dock," *Chronicle of Higher Education,* 21 July 2000.

10   Ben Gose, "Brandeis Wins Legal Dispute over Its Handling of Date-Rape Charge," *Chronicle of Higher Education,* 6 October 2000.

Chapter 5

1   David. C. Geary, *Male, Female: The Evolution of Human Sex Differences* (Washington, D.C.: American Psychological Association, 1998), p. 315.

2   Kelly Ryan, "PSAT Exam Changing to Remedy Bias Claims," *Dallas Morning News,* 15 October 1996.

3   Linda Chavez, testimony before the House Education and Workforce Committee, Subcommittee on Oversight and Investigations, 22 June 1999.

4   "Little Is Changed in Latest Draft of Education Department Guidelines on Standardized Tests," *Chronicle of Higher Education,* 14 July 2000.

5   General Accounting Office, "Gender Equity: Men's and Women's Participation in Higher Education," Report to the Ranking Minority Member, Subcommittee on Criminal Justice, Drug Policy and Human Resources, Committee on Government Reform, House of Representatives, December 2000, p. 10.

6   David Sadker, "Gender Games," *Washington Post,* 30 July 2000.

7   U.S. Department of Education Office for Civil Rights, Draft Investigative Manual, Underrepresentation of Females and Minorities in Upper-Level Mathematics and Science, August 1994.

8   Investigators' interview with commissioners, United States Commission on Civil Rights, *Equal Educational Opportunity and Nondiscrimination for Girls in Advanced Mathematics, Science and Technology Education,* 1999, Introduction, p. 24.

9   *Equal Educational Opportunity and Nondiscrimination for Girls in Advanced Mathematics, Science and Technology Education,* ch. 8, p. 2.

10   Patricia Hausman, "A Bias Against Boys," *Washington Times,* 13 December 1999.

11   Scott Smallwood, "Report Questions Methodology and Conclusions of MIT Gender-Discrimination Study," *Chronicle of Higher Education,* 7 February 2001.

12   David Gelernter, "Women and Science at Yale," *Weekly Standard,* 21 June 1999.

13   Jack Chambers, "Schools Sidelined by Cheerleading Controversies," *Dallas Morning News,* 16 January 1994.

14   Ethan Bronner, "Lawsuit on Sex Bias by 2 Mothers, 17," *New York Times,* 6 August 1998.

15   Jay Johnson, "Physically Fit Students? Fat Chance?" *San Diego Union-Tribune,* 15 November 1984.

16   Abby Goodnough, "Gym Now Stresses Cooperation, Not Competition," *New York Times,* 5 July 2000.

17   Jack McCallum, "Gym Class Struggle," *Sports Illustrated,* 24 April 2000.

18   Gia Fenoglio, "The Price of Equality," *National Journal,* 17 March 2001.

Chapter 6

1   David C. Geary, *Male, Female: The Evolution of Human Sex Differences* (Washington, D.C.: American Psychological Association, 1998), p. 226.

2   Ibid., p. 214.

3   Ibid., p. 228.

4   Ibid., p. 235.

5   Eleanor E. Maccoby, *The Two Sexes: Growing Up Apart, Coming Together* (Cambridge: Harvard University Press, 1998), p. 38.

6   Ibid., p. 39.

7   Ibid., p. 45.

8   Ibid., p. 26.

9   Geary, *Male, Female,* p. 259.

10   Doreen Kimura, *Sex and Cognition* (Cambridge: MIT Press, 2000), p. 68; and Geary, *Male, Female,* p. 312.

11   Kimura, *Sex and Cognition,* p. 68.

12   Ibid., p. 43.

13   Geary, *Male, Female,* p. 263.

14   Ibid.

15   Kimura, *Sex and Cognition,* p. 77.

16   Ibid., p. 68.

17   Ibid., p. 62.

18   Andrew Sullivan, "The He Hormone," *New York Times Magazine*, 2 April 2000.

19   James McBride Dabbs (with Mary Godwin Dabbs), *Heroes, Rogues and Lovers: Testosterone and Behavior* (New York: McGraw-Hill, 2000), p. 60.

20   Ibid., p. 91.

21   Geary, *Male, Female*, p. 228.

22   Ibid.

23   Kate Zernike, "Girls a Distant 2nd in Geography Gap among U.S. Pupils," *New York Times*, 31 May 2000.

24   Geary, *Male, Female*, pp. 186–87.

25   Michael Lynch, "Title IX's Pyrrhic Victory," *Reason*, 1 April 2001.

Chapter 7

1   National Collegiate Athletic Association press release, "NCAA Gender-Equity Study Shows Small Gains for Women's Sports," 25 October 1999.

2   "Title IX and Women in Sports: What's Wrong with This Picture?" *National Desk*, PBS, 1999.

3   Welch Suggs, "Female Athletes Thrive, but Budget Pressures Loom," *Chronicle of Higher Education*, 18 May 2001.

4   James L. Shulman and William G. Bowen, *The Game of Life: College Sports and Educational Values* (Princeton: Princeton University Press, 2001), p. 131.

5   Ibid., p. 133.

6   Ibid., p. 145.

7   Ibid., p. 136.

8   Lena Williams, "Women's Sports Foundation Expands Mission Beyond Opening Doors," *New York Times*, 7 May 2000.

9   Paul Farhi, "They Got Game but Few Fans," *Washington Post*, 7 June 2001.

10   *All Things Considered*, National Public Radio, 27 July 2001.

INDEX